MW00326200

The Essence of Christian Doctrine

A Brief Study of the Apostles' Creed and Basic Christian Doctrine

Martin Murphy

Second Edition

The Essence of Christian Doctrine

Published by: Theocentric Publishing Group
1069A Main Street
Chipley, Florida 32428

http://www.theocentricpublishing.com

ISBN 9780984570812

To those who contributed to this work
By their sermons, lessons, and lectures
Especially Dr. Steve Brown who motivated me to write
The late Dr. John Gerstner who gave me a passion
For theological studies
Pastor James Vickery for his godly goading
And my wonderful wife Mary
Sine qua non

Preface

For most of my adult life it appeared to me that evangelical Christians look for reality in drama, music, and other highly visceral means of communication. For nearly fifty years I have observed the curtailment of rational thinking which results in the decrease of Christian doctrine finding a place in spiritual growth. Words like doctrine have taken the back seat to words like relationships. I heard a preacher say "the answer to the problems we face today is not found in Bible study, but in our relationships with each other." This brief study of the basic content of the Christian faith is unashamedly derived from biblical doctrine. Although sound doctrine is important, personal application is necessary to bring the doctrine alive. A deliberate attempt has been made to apply the doctrine with clarity and compelling conviction.

My purpose for publishing this book on the essential doctrine of the Christian religion is twofold. First I want to show that the Apostles' Creed is a basic statement of Christian doctrine. Secondly and most important I want Christians to know how to express their faith in simple terms but with meaningful reasons based on biblical teaching. I will take each section of the Apostles' Creed and show the biblical basis for the statement as well as meaningful application. The other chapters have been added to compliment the basic doctrine found in the Apostles' Creed.

Since the Western version of the Apostles' Creed is more commonly used by English speaking people, I will include it in the preface to the commentary.

APOSTLES' CREED

I believe in God the Father almighty, maker of heaven and earth; and in Jesus Christ his only Son, our Lord; Who was conceived by the Holy Ghost, born of the Virgin Mary, suffered under Pontius Pilate, was crucified, dead and buried; He descended into hell; the third day he rose again from the dead; He ascended into heaven, and sitteth on the right hand of God the Father almighty; from thence He shall come to judge the quick and the dead.

I believe in the Holy Spirit; the holy catholic church; the communion of the saints; the forgiveness of sins; the resurrection of the body; and the life everlasting.

Amen

Table of Contents

Christians Believe

The apostle Peter was one of the first in the New Testament church to establish a principle that has been used throughout the history of the church. In the gospel of John Peter said, "We have come to believe and know that You are the Christ, the Son of the living God" (John 6:69). It was one of the early creeds of the New Testament Church.

Creeds have always been important to Christians, so they should understand what creeds are and why they are important. A creed is a statement of one's belief. The English word creed comes from the Latin word *credo*, which means, "I believe." The English words "believe, trust, faith, and persuade" that are often found in the New Testament can be traced to the same family of Greek words. So when a person says "I believe" it may also be said that "I have faith, I trust, or I am persuaded."

Every rational human being has a creed, because it is impossible to live as a rational being without believing something. A collection of knowledge may be expressed in a creed. For example I have a creed which goes something like this: I believe the Bible is the inspired Word of God. I am making a statement based on a larger collection of information about the Bible. My statement is my creed and some people may say my creed is wrong. If so, further inquiry and study may cause me to revise my creed, although I have studied it for thirty years and so far no revision has been made.

Many people have creeds that appear contradictory to reality. For instance, someone may have a creed that sounds something like this: I believe little green Martians visit the earth occasionally. There is no evidence to believe such a creed. The power of suggestion is not sufficient to establish a creed. Christians above all people must not accept a creed simply because someone makes an assertion. Remember your creed is a summary of a greater body of knowledge. Peter's creed was based on his belief and knowledge that Christ was the Son of the living God.

The origin of Christian creeds can be traced to the need for instruction and preparation for a public profession of faith and baptism which matriculated them into the membership of the church. The early church insisted that new converts be able to confess their faith in clear succinct, but substantial terms. Those who applied for church membership were orally taught and expected to profess faith according to the creed based on the doctrine of the Bible placed in logical order. When someone was presented for baptism, which indicated membership in the church, some creeds emphasized "I believe" in an attempt to make the profession of faith personal. Other early creeds used the formula "we believe" to reflect the individual agreement with the church collectively. The majority of the Western church used "I believe". The majority of the Eastern Church used "we believe." Later the creeds were put in writing.

The Apostles' Creed is one of the most reliable and biblically consistent creeds still in use among many evangelical churches. The Apostles' Creed also has the benefit of expressing the fundamental historical theology and doctrine of evangelicalism. It begins with God the Creator and reveals the necessity of salvation by Jesus Christ who was born in history, lived and died, was resurrected in history and is now the Judge of history. Although Christians universally use the creed, it is not a complete body of the principles of truth found in the Word of God.

For that reason the church may use other creeds and confessions to clarify and expand the body of truth found in the Apostles' Creed. The Nicene Creed further explains the nature of the Trinity. The Athanasian and Chalcedon Creeds further explain the person, nature, and character of Jesus Christ. When someone recites the Apostles' Creed they are duty bound to explain its meaning and show the truthfulness and integrity of the creed based on the Word of God.

The content of the Apostles' Creed may not make sense unless there is a clear picture of what it means to have the ability to believe. The essence of any creedal formula begins with God as the sovereign and substance. God enables a person to believe.

> And on the Sabbath day we went outside the gate to a riverside, where we were supposing that there would be a place of prayer; and we sat down and began speaking to the women who had assembled. And a certain woman named Lydia, from the city of Thyatira, a seller of purple fabrics, a worshiper of God, was listening; and the Lord opened her heart to respond to the things spoken by Paul. (Acts16:13,14, NASB)

The Holy Spirit opens the heart to enable the sinner to believe. The power of the Holy Spirit renews the mind so that the truth of the Word of God can be believed. The Holy Spirit of God changes the will so that the truth of the Word of God can be acted upon. After God changes the heart, the converted sinner must then engage tirelessly in the noble work of inquiring into God's word. It is unreasonable and unthinkable that a person could believe the truth taught in the Word of God, if that person was ignorant of the Word of God.

One of the essential doctrines of evangelicalism is saving faith which consists of three constituent parts. Traditional evangelical theology used three Latin words to explain saving faith. The first word is *notitia* which involves the use of the mind. Faith must have content or the object of faith. The mind has knowledge of the object of faith. For instance, the mind must have some knowledge of God, before one is able to believe. The second word is *assensus*. It refers to the intellectual assent to the content of faith. For example, I not only have knowledge of God, but I assert there is a God. The third word is *fiducia* which means to trust the object of faith. This moves the unbeliever into the category of a believer. These distinctions are important because the Bible teaches that even Satan believes there is a gospel of grace and he has knowledge of the content, but he does not trust the object, the Lord Jesus Christ, for salvation.

Christians say, "I believe" with a full assent to the authority of God. Christians say, "I believe" because they love the truth found in the Word of God. Christians say "I believe" because they desire fellowship with the Savior. Faith and believing does not stand alone. The words belief, faith, and persuade belong to the same family originating from Greek and moving to Latin and then to English. When you say I believe you are essentially saying you have faith. It naturally follows that belief is an activity of the whole soul. If you believe, then you must have faith, and if you have faith you must have knowledge. It is impossible to assert any truth if utter ignorance prevails. There is an old maxim attributed to St. Hilary of the 5th century. "A person cannot express what he does not know and he cannot believe what he cannot express." Hilary's words agree with the words of our Lord in the gospel of John. "If I do not do the works of My Father, do not believe Me; but if I do them, though you do not believe Me, believe the works, that you may know and understand that the Father is in Me, and I in the Father" (John 10:37-38, NASB). Knowledge and understanding, no matter how limited it may be, will precede faith and belief. The Lord did not say believe without providing a reason to believe. Jesus persuaded the disciples by His works to prove that He was the Son of God. What was the means of persuasion? It was evidence. Paul explains the importance of evidence rather than attempting to eliminate it from the basic Christian doctrine (Acts 17:31).

An example of true faith is found in the gospel of Luke. It is the account of a Roman army officer who had called for Jesus to heal a household servant. When Jesus came to the home of the army officer, the officer said to Jesus, "Lord do not trouble Yourself, for I am not worthy that you should enter under my roof" (Luke 7:1-10). The army officer saw his insignificance in comparison to the worthiness of Jesus Christ. The army officer was a sinner aware of his need of the grace of God. The officer believed that Jesus Christ was the Son of God. The information or evidence convinced the army officer that Jesus could do what He said he could do.

Then Jesus responded to the crowd of unbelieving Jews and said: "I say to you, I have not found such great faith, not even in Israel." Why didn't Jesus find great faith in Israel? Faith will be measured to the sinner in relation to his need before God. Great faith comes from a great need. Israel was self-righteous and

5

had no need for faith. On the other hand, the sinner is aware of his need of the righteousness of Jesus Christ. Are you in great need? If so God will measure great faith to you.

God

The Apostles' Creed begins with "I believe in God the Father almighty maker of heaven and earth." For over twenty years I taught, lectured, defended and preached about God the Father almighty maker of heaven and earth in a variety of places. I have asked hundreds of people this question, "How would you describe God?" The answers were amazing! Many would say "God is the supreme being" or "God is love." None of those adequately describe God, but are merely aspects of His being.

The Apostles' Creed refers to the doctrine of the Trinity without using the word Trinity. This section teaches the doctrine of God, the first person of the Trinity. Other sections teach the doctrine of Jesus Christ, the second person of the Trinity, and the doctrine of the Holy Spirit, the third person of the Trinity.

Unfortunately, many professing Christians say "I believe in God," but know little if anything about Him. World religions and many religious organizations, like the Masons, refer to their god as a supreme being and they see him as the source of love. It is impossible to fully describe the nature and character of God, but the children's catechism has an excellent answer that summarizes the description we find of God in the Bible. What is God? "God is a Spirit, infinite, eternal, and unchangeable in His being, wisdom, power, holiness, justice, goodness, and truth" (*Westminster Shorter Catechism*).

God is Spirit and with Him being spiritual, it is not unusual for Christians to abstain from contemplating the spiritual dimension because of their insecurity.

They are insecure because they are dependent beings, therefore dependent on God who is Spirit.

Some of the fundamental principles of the spiritual dimension are almost ignored, such as the self existence of God. Many individual Christians and much of the contemporary church have little interest in the magnificent doctrine known as the self-existence of God. Christians ought to learn and use the word aseity because it describes the self-existent independent being of God. God cannot be the cause of Himself; therefore He is independent in all His perfections. That means God is the source of all being, both material and spiritual. As the inspired apostle Paul said, "In Him we live and move and have our being" (Acts 17:28). A misunderstanding of God's nature and character has caused the church to split into a thousand pieces. Unless Christians understand the fundamental doctrine of God, they will never be able to agree on other biblical doctrine or effectively share the grace of God with unbelievers.

I want to give you a brief picture of God the Father almighty maker of Heaven and Earth. I have heard professing Christians say, "I can't discuss religion with such and such." Both people claim to be Christians. If they are not able to discuss their religion with one another they are liars if they both say, "I believe in God the Father almighty." If they are not able to discuss their belief in God and what it means to profess faith in God, then there is no common "God the Father among them." If God is our Father, we (the children of God) cannot have but one Father.

Using the word Father to address the true and living God may communicate different things to different people. Think about your father. What kind of man was he? How did he treat you? What was his character like? What about his relationship to his wife and to you? If you had never seen a Bible and never heard biblical teaching about God the Father, the word "father" would and probably still does in some sense, bring to your mind an image of your earthly father. You may know something about the meaning of the word father based on your experience however it may not express the nature and character of God the Father. Christians have to put aside all those thoughts and start over thinking in terms of God the Father from a biblical perspective. Since Christians have one common heavenly Father, they should refer to Him as "our Father." Jesus taught his disciples to pray in terms of "our" Father, not "my" Father (Luke 11:2). The following is a brief description of our Father:

> Our heavenly Father is sovereign, dignified above all other personalities, and demonstrates the most excellent divine perfections that can be imagined (Isaiah 6:1-3).

> Our heavenly Father is the perfect Father (Matthew 5:48).

> Our heavenly Father is the most wise Father (1 Timothy 1:17).

> Our heavenly Father is the most loving Father (1 John. 4:16).

> Our heavenly Father has unsearchable riches (Colossians 1:16).

> Our heavenly Father truly understands and applies the doctrine of forgiveness. If the guilt of sin is not

forgiven and the particular sins are not forgiven, you will forever be tormented in your soul (Ephesians 4:32).

Our heavenly Father is the best Father, because He can reform His children (Acts 16:14).

Our heavenly Father will polish His children and make them shining vessels to His glory (Isaiah 60:1).

Our heavenly Father is the oldest Father in the Universe (Daniel 7:9).

Our heavenly Father lives forever (Isaiah 57:15).

If you have true faith, you must believe that God is your Father. If I have true faith, I must believe that God is my Father, so we both say "our" Father.

Although the doctrine of God is large and not studied as it ought to be, there are three concepts of His being that are essential for the Christian religion. Every Christian should learn these terms because they are the foundation for all other Christian doctrine. Christians ought to memorize these words: omnipotence, omnipresence, and omniscience.

God is not only our Father, He is our Father almighty. The word omnipotence means "all powerful." Dr. John Gerstner would often say "God is not some mighty, He is *ALL* mighty. When we say that God is almighty, we mean that He is all powerful. Through the centuries there have been professing Christians attempting to deny God of His rightful power. When we say that we believe that God is almighty, we are merely saying what Scripture says.

"Whatever the Lord pleases, He does, in heaven and in earth, in the seas and in all deep places. He causes the vapors to ascend from the ends of the earth; He makes lightning for the rain; He brings forth the wind out of His treasuries (Psalm 135:6-7).

God is almighty in the sense that He not only can do what He wills to do, but He actually does what He wills to do. God's power and might is such that He is not capricious. God is immutable or to put it another way God's nature and character always has been and always will be the same. The inspired words of the apostle Paul remind us that God works all things after the counsel of His will (Ephesians 1:11). Therefore Christians understand that God Almighty is without limits or bounds, either actual or possible. God is all sufficient. Nothing can be added to or taken away from God in all His perfections.

God is present everywhere at one time. As the Psalmist says "Where can I flee from Your presence" (Psalm 139:7). This is one of the three cardinal doctrines of God, also known by the term omnipresence. It refers to God's being "everywhere present at once." It is often said that the worst part of being in Hell is that God would not be there. Is it possible for God to be everywhere and not be everywhere at the same time? If that was true, then God would be contradictory and no longer possess the characteristics that belong to God. It is the independent, infinite, and spiritual nature of God that causes Him to be everywhere at once. God will be in Heaven demonstrating His love and grace, but He will be in Hell in an unfavorable way demonstrating His wrath.

God is omniscient which means that God is "all knowing." God not only knows everything, He never forgets anything. I've heard people say "when God forgives our sins, He forgets them." That is not true. God is incapable of forgetting, but out of His vast grace He chooses not to bring the sins up again. Some of God's attributes are His perfect Excellencies such as wisdom, holiness, goodness, grace, and justice. Just think, God judges without prejudice.

Another aspect of God's character is the incomprehensible nature of God. Christians cannot know everything about God for as Scripture reveals "To whom then will you liken God? Or what likeness will you compare to Him?" (Isaiah 40:18). The apostle Paul asked the rhetorical question, "Who has known the mind of the Lord?" (Romans 11:34). We may know enough about God to worship Him and glorify Him, but we must not probe to know more than God has chosen to reveal about Himself.

Since God made heaven and earth, He must be eternal. He is without beginning and He has no end. It is said that God created or made the world out of nothing. It should be corrected to say God did not use any pre-existing substance to create the world. He created out of His own power and from His independent character; He created a dependent creation. The doctrine of creation gives us a glimpse into the law of causality. God was the first independent cause, and everything that follows depends on that first independent cause. The law of causality describes the relationship between cause and its effect. Every effect must have a *sufficient* cause. It is a practical application of the law of non-contradiction. God is independent of creation thus it may be said that God is the first cause of all things. The Bible teaches that God ordained everything that has or will ever happen. His ordination included the instruments and occasions which are called second causes. For example, God the first cause ordained that the apple would fall to the ground, but He also ordained gravity which is the second cause to bring about the apple falling to the ground. Chapter fifteen has more to say about God's eternal plan and creation.

The being and character of God is so evident that every Christian should gladly say, "God the Father Almighty is our Creator, our owner, and benefactor in whom we live and move and have our being." The next time you publicly profess to believe in God the Father Almighty consider the dignity and honor you have by being able to call the true and living God our God the Father almighty. His love and affection will over-whelm you. His wisdom will teach you. He will provide all your needs.

Jesus said to a group of Pharisees, "You are of your father the devil and the desires of your father you want to do" (John 8:44). Remember they wanted to kill Jesus. Those Pharisees represent unbelievers who profess to believe God, so it should be noticed accord-ing to this text, that unbelievers have Satan as their father. He teaches them how to live, deceive, and destroy.

Believers on the other hand have God the Father almighty maker of heaven and earth. He teaches them how to live truthfully with honor, dignity, and peace. God is very near, but in heaven He takes delight in your confession; "God the Father almighty maker of heaven and earth."

Jesus Christ

There are four titles assigned to the second person of the Trinity according to the Apostles' Creed.

1. Jesus
2. Christ
3. The only Son
4. Lord

The origin and meaning of these titles, as with any other biblical doctrine, requires diligent attention to the full counsel of God. The disciple of Christ must study the corresponding relationships used in both the Old Testament and the New Testament. These corresponding relationships are called types. For instance a good Bible student will examine a person in the Old Testament to help establish parallels and similarities to people in the New Testament. If in their study of the Bible they dismiss the use of types, they will suffer the peril of misinterpreting the Word of God. All the titles of the second person of the Trinity used in the Apostles' Creed have types in the Old Testament.

The first title is Jesus. From the Old Testament the name Jesus is derived from a Hebrew word meaning salvation or deliverer. For example, Joshua the son of Nun is an Old Testament type of Jesus, the deliverer. The title Jesus has a variety of applications, but the name Jesus places emphasis on the humanity of the second person of the Trinity. For instance that kind of language is found in the gospel of Matthew. "And she will bring forth a Son, and you shall call His name Jesus, for He will save His people from their sins" (Matthew 1:21). In order to save His people He had to physically die on the cross, a substitutionary atonement, for their inherited sin nature and their actual sins.

The second title found in the Apostles' Creed is Christ. The Old Testament Messiah corresponds with Christ. It literally means the anointed one. The anointing of Christ signifies the office of mediator. Christ is a title that encompasses the Mediator with the inherent quality to intercede between holy God and sinful man. Christ is the antitype of the priest in the Old Testament. The priest was a representative for the people of God by offering sacrifices pleasing to God. However, the priest was sinful. Christ is the perfect priest. It is appropriate to call Christ the preeminent priest. The Book of Hebrews describes Christ not only offering a sacrifice; He offered a perfect sacrifice as one offering of Himself once for all (Hebrews chapter 10).

The third title "His only Son" reflects the relationship between the first person of the Trinity, God the Father, and second person of the Trinity, God the Son. The phrase "God's only Son" is another way of saying Jesus Christ was unique; He was and is one of a kind. The gospel of John refers to "the only begotten" which brings out the distinctive nature of being "His only Son" (John 1:14).

The fourth title given to the second person of the Trinity is Lord and it is the highest title known to man. The inspired apostle Paul explains the import of the title "Lord" in Philippians 2:9-11.

> Therefore God also has highly exalted Him and given Him the name which is above every name, that at the name of Jesus every knee should bow, of those in heaven, and of those on earth, and of those under the earth, and that every tongue

should confess that Jesus Christ is Lord, to the glory of God the Father. (Philippians 2:9-11).

It is worthy to notice that Jesus Christ humbled himself, but God the Father exalted Jesus Christ. In connection with that humility and exaltation God gave Christ the name above all names. His name is Lord.

The word "Lord" in the New Testament is translated from the Greek word *kurios*. The early Christians living under the rule of the Roman Empire could say Jesus or Christ and not get in trouble with the state. However, they had to be careful with the use of the word Lord. In fact the Roman Emperor used the word Lord to describe himself. During public gatherings the creedal formula was along the lines of publicly professing that Caesar was Lord. Naturally, Christians refused to say Caesar was Lord, but they would say Jesus is Lord. If the Christians refused to repent, it may cost them their lives. The Old Testament name for Lord is Yahweh or Jehovah, therefore the name Lord is the name that properly belongs to God himself. Some of the most sober, but yet awesome words ever recorded in Holy Scripture are found in the book of Philippians. Scripture affirms that "every knee will bow and every tongue will confess that Jesus Christ is Lord" (Philippians 2:10-11). Believers will bow because of their love and adoration for the Lord. Believers will humble themselves. Unbelievers will bow at the mighty sovereign hand of God and He will humble unbelievers since they will not humble themselves.

When Christians say, "we believe in Jesus Christ the Lord," a humble thankful heart is necessary to stand before God in His favorable presence to proclaim the name above all names. Those four titles, Jesus, Christ, Lord, and only Son characterize the fullness of the humanity and deity of the second person of the Trinity. Those titles bring to light the humiliation of Jesus, the exaltation of Christ, and the magnification of the Lord. These biblical concepts are further explained in this exposition of the Apostles' Creed.

Christians should ponder the mysterious phrase "the word became flesh" written by the apostle John in his gospel. When the Bible says Jesus Christ became flesh, it is a reference to Jesus Christ, the second person of the Trinity. To put it another way Jesus Christ was fully God and He was fully man. The Nicene Creed asserts that Jesus Christ is "of the same essence as the Father." Christ was divine in every way and He was human in every way, but without sin. His humanity began in a rather unique way. The Bible teaches that Jesus Christ was born of a virgin. His virgin birth was necessary for Him to be born without a sin nature. It was necessary for Christ to be free of sin in order to satisfy God's wrath. Without the unique virgin birth there is no hope of eternal salvation.

Jesus Christ was full of grace, which means He was filled with unmerited favor for the benefit of guilty sinners. The terms grace or unmerited favor needs some further explanation. Grace is a gift. You cannot demand grace or work for grace. As the old saying goes, there are no strings attached to grace.

Jesus is not only full of grace, He is full of truth. The word "truth" is used nearly 200 times in the Word of God. Any meaningful definition of the word truth will require a serious and resolute study of the whole counsel of God. The Bible defines itself as truth. "The entirety of Your word *is* truth, and every one of Your righteous judgments endures forever" (Psalm 119:160).

Christians must use the Bible as the point of reference to discover and understand truth. I know plenty of professing Christians who do not like the idea of absolute truth. Survey after survey has proven many professing Christians reject the idea of absolute truth. The Bible explains why unbelievers reject absolute truth. The truth is that unbelievers "exchange the truth of God for a lie" (Romans 1:25). We live in a world of liars, but the Bible declares that there is absolute and ultimate truth. It is found in Jesus Christ. "I am the way, the truth, and the life" (John 14:6). The living truth, the Lord Jesus Christ, gave His people the written truth which is the Word of God to stand against the lies of Satan.

Those who come to Christ are born, not of blood, nor of the will of the flesh, nor the will of man, but of God. It is the spiritual birth by an act of God and the applied righteousness of Christ by the power of the Holy Spirit that changes the sinner's spiritual condition. Those who have received this spiritual birth will gladly receive the Lord Jesus Christ. If you have received this spiritual birth, you will be able to say like the apostle John said "we beheld His glory, the glory as of the only begotten of the Father, full of grace and truth" (John 1:14).

Humiliation of Jesus Christ

The Apostles' Creed affirms that "Jesus Christ Suffered under Pontius Pilate, was crucified, dead and buried; He descended into hell." This expression may be properly explained as the humiliation of Jesus Christ. His life of suffering, His crucifixion and death are all acts of humiliation. The orthodox view of the second person of the Godhead, Jesus Christ, is that He is the one and only "fully God and yet fully man." For God to assume the nature of man was an act of humiliation. However, it is wrong to think or believe that God gave up any of His attributes to become man. The popular hymn "And Can It Be That I Should Gain" makes the assertion that Christ "emptied himself of all but love." That is simply not true and can lead someone into heresy. His humanity did not rob Him of His deity. Jesus Christ is unique in that He is one person with two natures: divine and human. This may be a mystery to the sinful finite human mind, but it is completely agreeable with the Word of God and sound reason. Although the Lord Jesus Christ remained God, it was an act of humiliation to assume the human nature. This essential doctrine of the life and work of Jesus Christ should be remembered as the doctrine of humiliation.

The Apostles' Creed refers to the suffering of Jesus Christ in terms of human suffering. Since His suffering was voluntary and only for the benefit of others, it is the purest form of humiliation. The beginning of His life is marked by bearing the form of a servant (Philippians 2:7) and appearing in the likeness of sinful flesh (Romans 8:3).

In His public ministry He suffered poverty and was treated with envy, malice, and reproach. Then at the end of His life He suffered beyond human comprehension for the sake of those who believe in His name. Why did He suffer? His purpose was to reconcile believers to God through Christ (2 Corinthians 5:18). His love for those whom God calls to Himself exceeds human understanding. The suffering of Jesus Christ was the ultimate sacrifice. "Greater love has no one than this, than to lay down one's life for his friends" (John 15:13).

The love Christ demonstrated by His humiliation should give every Christian joy, hope, and peace. The suffering and further humiliation of Christ was necessary for God to reconcile sinners to Himself so they are enabled to experience peace. How many times do Christians ignore His suffering by refusing to be reconciled to other Christians? The doctrine of reconciliation is not difficult to understand, but it is difficult to practice.

Crucifixion was a form of torture and execution for slaves and criminals in the Roman Empire. The sinless perfect man, the Lord Jesus Christ, suffered this cruel punishment and execution. It is called cruel punishment and execution, because it was nothing less. The typical Roman crucifixion consisted of three parts. First the condemned man was severely beaten before he was attached to the Cross. Then the condemned man had to carry his own cross to the place of execution. Finally the condemned man was stripped of his clothes and hung naked on the cross until he died.

Think of the humiliation of being exposed in the public square. The God of heaven and earth gladly endured this humiliation for the sake of those whom God has called to Himself. The crucifixion was merely a means to an end. To put this in perspective consider Paul's letter to the Romans. "But God demonstrates His own love toward us, in that while we were yet sinners, Christ died for us" (Romans 5:8).

Just before His human body expired, the Lord Jesus said, "It is finished" (John 19:30). It represents the final work of Jesus Christ by providing the perfect sacrifice to God the Father. The gospel of Luke says "Father into Thy hands I commit my spirit" (Luke 23:46). The work, which the Father had committed to His earthly life, was complete. The sinless man Jesus Christ suffered to the point of death. His sacrifice typified in the Old Testament was required to satisfy God's justice. Even though His death was the most horrible crime ever committed, it was necessary for the sake of saving His people (Matthew 1:21).

The death of Christ was and remains the only perfect sacrifice that satisfies God's wrath. It is a magnificent doctrine of the Christian religion. It is the only aspect of His life that Christians are commanded to celebrate. The Bible does not command the celebration of the birth of Christ or the numerous other celebrations orchestrated by the church. The Bible does command the child of God to celebrate the death of Jesus Christ. If this brings pause to your thoughts, examine the Word of God. "Do this in remembrance of Me" (Luke 22:19; also see Matthew 26:26-30; 1 Corinthians 11:26-28). This commandment is just as valid as the Ten Commandments. Christians are commanded to celebrate His death by remembering Him.

His burial, as any human burial, brings closure to earthly life. Death ends human life, but burial closes the human experience by removing the bodily remains from our sight. The burial was conducted honorably following the tradition of the Jews. The Bible speaks of burial over 100 times. The Bible says Abraham buried his wife "out of his sight" (Genesis 23:4). Death and burial are important aspects of God's eternal plan.

The crucifixion, death, and burial did not end the suffering of Jesus Christ. The Apostles' Creed describes the humiliation of the Lord Jesus Christ in Hellish terms. The Creed describes His humiliation in terms of His descent into hell. This little phrase, "He descended into hell," found in the Apostles' Creed has long been a point of contention for some Christians. It is sufficient to say that His descent into hell is not the same thing as suffering the hellishness of this life. The Creed has already dealt adequately with that aspect of Christ's suffering. The Lord's descent into Hell could not be His death and burial for those truths precede His descent into hell according to the creed. Then what does it mean? This part of the creed signifies the exponential horrors, agony, pain, and anguish suffered by the Lord Jesus Christ. His soul was tormented greater than anyone can imagine, so that His suffering exceeded any other human being. *The Heidelberg Catechism* is most helpful. Question 44 asks, "Why is there added, he descended into hell." Answer: "That in my greatest temptations, I may be assured, and wholly comfort myself in this, that my Lord Jesus Christ, by his inexpressible anguish, pains, terrors, and hellish agonies, in which he was plunged during all his sufferings, but especially on the cross, hath delivered me from the anguish and torments of hell." Jesus Christ suffered the pain of hell for all those whom God calls to Himself.

The humiliation of the Lord Jesus Christ was for true believers. Humility belongs to those who belong to Jesus Christ. Humility is a mark of the true believer

24

and humility should accompany them and be their posture before a holy redeeming Savior. The opposite of humility is pride. The Puritan preacher, Thomas Manton, said "pride is a lifting up of the heart above God and against God and without God." Another Puritan preacher said "pride loves to climb up, not as Zaccheus to see Christ, but to be seen." The sin of pride is a chief sin. The proud think they are above others in position and rank in life. God will eventually bring down the proud and arrogant. Jeremiah the prophet said, "Behold, I am against you, O most haughty one! says the Lord God of hosts; For your day has come, the time that I will punish you" (Jeremiah 50:31ff). It should be observed from Scripture that the Lord punishes the proud and arrogant, but the Lord rescues the humble by His service of humiliation.

It is not enough that Christians repeat by memory the Apostles' Creed therefore professing to believe the doctrine of the humiliation of Jesus Christ, but also to endeavor to understand that doctrine. This brief exposition of the text touches the high points, but everyone who believes this doctrine must labor to understand it. It will give you confidence that your eternal home is heaven (Colossians 1:3-5). You will have the joy of the Lord in your life (1 Peter 1:8). The benediction from the Lord Jesus Christ is "peace be with you" (John 20:19, 21, 26).

Exaltation of Jesus Christ

Since the Apostles' Creed is a brief statement that explains the fundamental doctrine of the Christian religion, it should be an aid to help answer the universal question, "where am I going?" How many times have you heard someone say "when you die, it's all over?" Death does not equal nothingness, despite the contention of so many liberal Christians and atheists. The Jewish Sect of the Sadducees during the Lord's earthly ministry denied the resurrection of the body.

The Apostles' Creed teaches what Scripture teaches on this subject. "I believe Jesus Christ rose again on the third day from the dead and ascended into heaven." The birth, life, crucifixion, death, and burial of Jesus Christ define the doctrine of His humiliation. The resurrection and ascension describes the exaltation of Jesus Christ. His resurrection was the point of transition from His state of humiliation to His state of exaltation. Both, the doctrine of humiliation and exaltation, are found in Paul's first letter to the Corinthian Church in the fifteenth chapter.

Jesus Christ was crucified, dead, and buried. Only a few would deny that truth. However, many deny that He bodily rose from the dead. They do not believe His resurrection was real. Most people are fascinated with the thought of the resurrection. Some people are fascinated with the power of the resurrection. The most fascinating and mysterious aspect of the resurrection has to do with a new body. The resurrection is something Christians should think about daily because it is the centerpiece of the Christian religion.

Even though all four gospel accounts explain the truth of the empty tomb and the resurrection of

Christ, many try to explain away that truth. Some say that the disciples simply stole the body from the tomb and the Roman guards were paid to say it happened while they slept. I ask the rational mind, how did they know the body was stolen if they were asleep? Others say Jesus did not die, but only fainted and was revived by the cool tomb in which Jesus was laid. My response is that the soldiers found Jesus dead which is the reason they did not break His legs. Others say that the disciples only saw visions of the resurrected body of Christ. I ask you, is it characteristic for God to deceive people with visions? Then there are those who believe the resurrection was mythological. It was a spiritual resurrection. If so, then everything that happened to Christ is a myth and the Christian religion is a myth.

The poor soul that does not have hope in the resurrection of the body dismisses an essential doctrine of the Christian religion. The inspired words of the apostle Paul were spoken to the church of God, not to unbelievers. "If in this life only we have hope in Christ, we are of all men the most pitiable" (1 Corinthians 15:19). The word "pitiable" could be translated from the Greek text as "miserable." Paul simply expresses the pathetic and sorrowful condition of Christians if there is no hope for the resurrection of the body. The resurrection of Jesus Christ gives Christians the hope, not only the hope, but the promise of the resurrection.

Christians believe and hope in the resurrection because the evidence for the resurrection corresponds with reality. There is no reason not to believe the real historical account of Paul meeting Jesus on the road to Jericho.

As he journeyed he came near Damascus, and sud-
denly a light shone around him from heaven. Then
he fell to the ground, and heard a voice saying to
him, "Saul, Saul, why are you persecuting Me?"
And he said, "Who art Thou, Lord?" And He said,
"I am Jesus whom you are persecuting..." (Acts
9:3-5).

Later when Paul wrote the Corinthian Church
and said "Christ has been raised from the dead" (1
Corinthians 15:20), he is not speaking out of ignorance
and confusion. He actually saw the Lord Jesus Christ
after the ascension. Paul had been in contact with the
twelve apostles and other disciples of Christ who had
seen Christ crucified, die on the cross, buried in the
grave and raised on the third day. Paul knew the
teaching of the Old Testament and was aware of the
prophecies of Jesus Christ. The evidence for the
resurrection of Christ compelled Paul to preach "Jesus
and the resurrection" (Acts 17:18). The apostle would
have been mentality deranged to deny the resurrection
of the Lord Jesus Christ. Paul argues that the resurrection of Jesus Christ corresponds with reality (See 1
Corinthians 15).
The doctrine of the exaltation of Jesus Christ is
the sure hope and confidence for Christians. The
doctrine is also necessary for the great evangelistic
enterprise of the Christian church. The unique message
of the Christian evangelistic enterprise is the resurrection of the Lord Jesus Christ. Christianity stands alone
among all the world religions because of the promise of
the resurrection. A good hymn of praise for every
worship service is:

Up from the grave He arose,

With a mighty triumph o'er His foes;'
He arose a Victor from the dark domain,
And He lives forever with His saints to reign.
He arose! He arose!
Hallelujah! Christ arose!

Many Christians celebrate the resurrection of the Lord Jesus Christ at least once a year during the Easter holiday. When should the church celebrate the resurrection of Jesus Christ? The early church fathers taught that Christians should assemble together on the day of the resurrection commonly known as the first day of the week and celebrate His resurrection. To put it in plain language, the early church celebrated His resurrection every Lord's day not just once a year at the Easter festival. The reason Christians assemble together in worship to read the Bible, pray, sing praises, and take the Lord's Supper is to worship the resurrected Lord. What a privilege to worship the Lord with the doctrine that affirms the resurrection; "We believe Jesus Christ rose again on the third day from the dead and ascended into heaven." The resurrection often finds its way into our religious conversations, but the ascension is rarely mentioned except in the Apostles' Creed. So much is said about the resurrection of Jesus Christ that His ascension almost becomes obscure, but Holy Scripture is not silent. The gospel of Luke describes the ascension. "And He led them out as far as Bethany, and He lifted up His hands and blessed them. Now it came to pass, while He blessed them, that He was parted from them and carried up into heaven" (Luke 24:50-51). The book of Acts describes the event in similar terms. "Now when He had spoken these things, while they watched, he was taken up, and a cloud received Him out of their sight" (Acts 1:9).

The ascension of Christ represents the accomplishment of His mission on earth. There is a biblical principle in the ascension that should delight the heart of every Christian. The principle is that exaltation follows humiliation. The doctrine of the ascension explains the transition from His humble earthly ministry to His exalted heavenly ministry. The ascension is a significant aspect of His exaltation and enthronement at the right hand of the Father.

The apostles representing the church nearly 2000 years ago mused at the ascension of the Lord Jesus Christ. In contrast to that solemn occasion on the Mount of Olives, many leaders in the contemporary church are amusing God's people with the ascension of man-centered worship, man-centered doctrine, and man made solutions to the confusion in this world. The word "muse" refers to meditation and most often a state of profound meditation. The word "amuse" is often used in terms of entertainment, most often with a comical aspect. The apostles gazed at the marvelous transition of the second person of the Trinity, while the contemporary church often entertains itself with imagery that does not portray the truth of the Word of God.

Jesus has been exalted into the highest heavens. The powerful presence of the Holy Spirit among Christians gives them an intimate and personal communion with the exalted Lord. The Lord Jesus Christ descended from heaven from the spiritual realms of the Triune God, but He ascended into heaven with a sinless human nature. He is there now preparing a mansion for His people for their glorified bodies, where there is no suffering, no sorrow, no pain, no sickness, and no death. Christians will rejoice when they see the heavens opened and the Son of Man standing at the right hand of God. The Christian church collectively says "we believe that Jesus Christ, the Lord of heaven and earth and the savior of sinners was exalted when He rose again from the dead and ascended into heaven."

Enthronement of Jesus Christ

The book of Hebrews is a good beginning point to better understand the doctrine that Jesus Christ sits on the right hand of God the Father Almighty. "But this Man, after He had offered one sacrifice for sins forever, sat down at the right hand of God, from that time waiting till His enemies are made His footstool. For by one offering He has perfected forever those who are being sanctified" (Hebrews 10:12-14).

The language found in the book of Hebrews describes the picture of Christ assuming His position at the right hand of God. I want to consider three aspects of the enthronement of Jesus Christ. First the Bible says Jesus "sat down" then "He sat at the right hand" and finally it was at "the right hand of God" (Hebrews 10:12).

The fact that He sat down indicates that He had completed His work of atonement on earth and began His work of intercession in heaven. The Old Testament priests stood daily offering sacrifices. It was a continual process of work standing day after day, until Jesus Christ finally completed the work and sat down at the right hand of God. The proper place of the servant is to stand and the master to sit. During His earthly humiliation the Lord Jesus Christ was a servant. Isaiah further clarifies the concept by describing Jesus Christ in terms of a suffering servant (Isaiah 52:13 – 53:12). The picture of His work on earth is one of standing, but in heaven He sits like a master. Sitting is a sign of judicial and royal authority. Christ is our master and He is the final authority of all faith and life for the Christian.

The second aspect of the enthronement of Jesus Christ is His position in heaven with relation to God the Father. The writer of Hebrews said Jesus Christ "sat down at the right hand of God." In ancient near eastern history sitting at the right hand is a metaphor that refers to a place of honor. When a king wanted to honor someone he would call that person to sit at his right hand which was the highest place of honor without exalting the other person above the king. This expression does not make Christ superior to the Father, but places Christ in an equal expression with the divine nature of God. Jesus Christ is at the proper place of full authority making redemption and the eternal home sure and unchangeable for those who belong to Him.

Now we come to the final aspect of the enthronement of Jesus Christ. His place is not only one of honor and authority, His place is with God the Father almighty. The gospel of John begins with these words: "In the beginning was the Word and the Word was with God and the Word was God" (John 1:1). When Christians confess that Jesus Christ sits on the right hand of God the Father Almighty, they acknowledge that Christ has returned to be with God as He was in the beginning, but now with a human nature.

The meaning of Christ sitting on the right hand of God does not just mean that Christ has merely forgiven the sinner and reconciled the broken relationship with God. Christ sits at the right hand of God as intercessor for the saved sinner. He is the Mediator between sinful man and holy God. Every moment Christ continues to reconcile the saved sinner to God. His exalted estate as a Mediator has three aspects. He is prophet, priest, and king.

The promise of the prophetic office of Jesus Christ was mentioned during the time of Moses. "The

Lord your God will raise up for you a prophet like me from your midst, from your brethren, Him you shall hear" (Deuteronomy.18:15). The Old Testament prophets anticipated the coming of the ultimate prophet, which was fulfilled in Jesus Christ. The word prophet in the New Testament comes from two Greek words which essentially means "to speak forth." The essence and use of the word prophet in the Bible is not about some master prognosticator. The biblical prophet is primarily a preacher and teacher. He speaks forth the word from the Lord. The earthly ministry of the Lord Jesus Christ was an active preaching and teaching ministry. Jesus did not spend most His time making predictions about what would happen in the future, but rather spent His time showing the world that He was full of grace and truth.

His work as the ultimate prophet is by revealing the will of God for the salvation of His people. The primary sources that reveal the way of salvation are the reading, studying, and meditating on the Word of God. Then He provides the preaching and teaching ministry. Sadly the preaching and teaching ministry has fallen on hard times, because so many preachers and teachers have taken the easy road. Many are not willing to do the hard work of biblical exegesis and exposition. By the grace of God there are theologians and Bible scholars who are capable and willing to preach and teach the word. Unfortunately there are numerous theologians and church doctors that do not believe the Bible and concoct a theology contrary to the Bible. Then there are those who become idols and heap up for themselves many followers by means of television or alleged Bible conferences. Then there are those who read the Bible for themselves and draw conclusions based on their preconceived ideas about the text. They claim to be open to Word of God, but fail to compare their views with the clear teaching of Scripture which leads to a distorted application. The Lord Jesus Christ has given His Word, so His people might be full of His words.

Secondly, Jesus Christ intercedes in the office of priest. "For Christ did not enter a holy place made with hands, a mere copy of the true one, but into heaven itself, now to appear in the presence of God for us" (Hebrews 9:24, NASB). Christ appears in the presence of God on behalf of those who are saved by His grace. Josephus and the writings of other Hebrew theologians reveal that the outer courts of the tabernacle were symbolical of the earth, and the holy of holies was symbolic of heaven. As it is, Jesus is in the most holy place, the holy of holies, in heaven interceding for His people. The people are in the outer court, this present world, confessing their sins and professing their belief in the almighty God of heaven and earth. While Christians confess their sins and profess their belief in almighty God, it is Jesus Christ who is at the right hand of God, interceding for them.

The sacrifice and intercession of Christ is essential if Christians expect to have a sense of God's presence with them. There are two dangers to avoid when considering the priestly office of Jesus Christ.

First, liberal theology essentially says the sacrifice of Christ is dead. There is no power in the gospel. They say we are intelligent and social beings and must continue the sacrifice that Christ started. Therefore the intercession by a dead Christ is not real.

Fundamentalist doctrine essentially teaches that the sacrifice of Jesus Christ was sufficient for potential salvation. To put it another way Jesus Christ died to make salvation possible. This view of intercession ultimately leads to "easy believism." Ask God for anything; believe it and it will happen. The word that best describes that view is *theantrophic*. It means a person has divine power because there is a little god within that person. If that is the case they do not need the intercession of Christ.

The biblical view of Jesus Christ as your high priest demonstrates that He is a real priest in time and eternity both now and in heaven. His sacrifice resulted in a living and all inclusive sacrifice. His sacrifice was not merely potential. He is acting on behalf of the ones He has redeemed and He sits at the right hand of God the Father almighty. How is it possible to enjoy a relationship with the High Priest in heaven? In all your consciousness be aware of His presence before God on your behalf and be aware that He is waiting on you to appear before Him in person to be received into glory.

Christ not only sits at the right hand of God as your prophet and priest, He is also your king. The kingdom of Christ is perpetual. It is not exclusively temporal or spiritual. "For the kingdom is the Lord's, And He rules over the nations" (Psalm 22:28). The Bible describes the spiritual nature in terms of everlasting. "Thy kingdom is an everlasting kingdom, and Thy dominion endures throughout all generations" (Psalm 145:13).

The kingdom of God includes the government of this world. When human government destroys our hopes and dreams, we look to the perfect Governor, Christ the King, to deliver us from the ruins of a sinful estate. We look for His kingship to bring order to this sin ruined world. The eternal or perpetual government of Jesus Christ depends, not on our good disposition, not on our ability to perfectly legislate morality, and not on our ability to rule the world. The perpetual government of Jesus Christ depends on His own power, authority, and sovereignty.

He gained the victory for Christians and will take them all the way into paradise where they will find Him sitting on the right hand of God the Father almighty.

Judgment by Jesus Christ

The Second Coming of Jesus Christ is a subject of great interest to Christians. The Apostles' Creed properly puts His second coming in the future. Paul's letter to Timothy refers to His second coming and judgment in terms of "His appearing" which implies a future event (See 2 Timothy 4:1-5).

How often do Christians consciously think about the second coming of Christ? I expect the answer is "probably not very often." Plans for family, work, social events, sports, or just mere leisure occupy the minds of Christians to the extent that any thought of the second coming takes very low priority in the thought life. They should think of His appearing often, because it is the great future hope of the Christian faith. It is true that the resurrection of the Lord Jesus Christ is the great hope, but the resurrection has already been accomplished. The second coming is the future hope. The promise of His return is found several places in Scripture, other than Paul's pastoral letter to Timothy. The promise for His return is found in the book of Acts. "This same Jesus, who was taken up from you into heaven, will so come in like manner as you saw Him go into heaven" (Acts 1:11).

The Apostles' Creed teaches that Jesus Christ will come again. The fundamental doctrine of His coming again is that Christ will return bodily. He ascended bodily into heaven. It was a physical ascent and it will be a physical descent. When He comes again in His body, it will be a visible return. The Book of Revelation promises that He will come "with clouds and every eye will see Him" (Revelation 1:7). His appearance will be the greatest eclipse of all times. The

Sun and all the stars of heaven will be dim in comparison to His appearance. His visible bodily return means that His appearing will be personal. The Lord said "If I go and prepare a place for you, I will come again and receive you to Myself; that where I am there you may be also" (John 14:3).

There is an element of mystery associated with His return because the Bible says everyone will see Him. Judas and all those who nailed Him to the cross will see Him. I do not think anyone on this planet can explain the details of His return, except God. He has chosen not to reveal them as of this writing. There is a connection with the doctrine of God's omnipresence (being everywhere present at once) and His return. It is a mystery and to question God shows a lack of faith in God's promises. For sure God does not make frivolous promises in His Word.

Another aspect of His appearing is that Jesus Christ will come gloriously with tens of thousands of angels. The host of heaven will proclaim His appearance. The Bible promises that He will come gloriously in flaming fire (2 Thessalonians 1:7), with the voice of the archangel and with the trumpet of God (1 Thessalonians 4:16). It will be the most glorious sight that mankind has ever seen. His bodily, visible, glorious return will be triumphant. He is the King of kings. He has won the battle and will return for His people having triumphed over His enemies.

It is certain He will return, but no earthly creature knows when He will return. His appearance will be unexpected. He will come in an hour unknown to anyone except the Triune God. He could come today while I am writing these words. All of our plans for this next week, next month, next year, or the next decade may disappear in an instant. The Bible says He will come like a thief in the night. Is there any reason to fear or tremble? It all depends on whether or not He has already come into your heart by the power of the Holy Spirit. His first appearance in the heart of man, figuratively speaking, is necessary for His second appearance to be in a favorable way.

If Jesus Christ has redeemed you, forgiven you of your sins and loved you with an everlasting love, there is every reason to rejoice in His bodily, visible, glorious, and triumphant return.

The promise of the second appearance of Jesus Christ is a very good reason to live godly lives. If we live this life without any restraint to the desires of the flesh, then we should examine ourselves to see if the first coming of Christ by the power of the Holy Spirit is really real. The promise of the second appearance of Christ should cause us to be patient and longsuffering during oppressions and afflictions in this life.

The Bible explains how He will come again, but why is He coming? He is coming to judge the quick and the dead. The biblical doctrine explains that He will judge both those who are alive and those who are dead. Obviously the creed is a mirror of Scripture at this point because Paul says "the Lord Jesus Christ who will judge the living and the dead at His appearing" (2 Timothy 4:1). There are other passages of Scripture that attest to the same doctrine. "For we must all appear before the judgment seat of Christ, that each one may receive the things done in the body, according to what he has done, whether good or bad" (2 Corinthians 5:10).

What does the Bible mean that everyone will appear before the judgment seat of Christ? The words "judgment seat" originally referred to a judicial bench. It literally refers to the bar of justice. The judgment seat is not a very good place to have to appear before, if the judgment seat implies a negative unfavorable place as it often seems to be from many references in Scripture. In fact the judgment seat is always used in a bad sense, except in Paul's letter to the Corinthians. For instance, Pilate was said to have sat on the judgment seat when he heard from Christ. For some strange reason, which I will never understand, many Christians do not think they will have to stand before the eternal Judge. They say once you become a Christian, there is no more judgment. Since the evidence from Scripture is so clear, I'll let God speak for Himself on this matter. A couple of Scripture references are sufficient to clarify any confusion.

Psalm 50:4 - He shall call to the heavens from above, And to the earth, that He may judge His people.

Romans 2:1 - God will judge the secrets of men by Christ Jesus.

Hebrews 10:30 - For we know Him who said, "Vengeance is Mine, I will repay" says the Lord. And again, "The Lord will judge His people."

The evidence in Scripture is powerfully persuasive. Christians will stand before the all-powerful divine Judge of heaven and earth. The gospel of Matthew plainly teaches that both the righteous and the wicked will appear in the judgment. The book of Revelation gives a vivid picture of the final judgment. "And I saw the dead the great and the small, standing before the throne, and books were opened; and another book was opened, which is the book of life; and the dead were judged from the things which were written in the books, according to their deeds" (Revelation 20:12).

The book of life will be opened during the process of the final judgment. It is difficult to be certain of the extent of this symbolism, but for sure the book of life is an absolute standard. It is not a matter of someone's opinion. The pure truth will be revealed from this book. First, the book of life is a test of ones legal standing with God. The question every person ought to ask is, "am I in a right relationship with God by grace through faith in Jesus Christ." Secondly the book of life measures the moral constitution, not from a human perspective, but as God sees it. Two more important questions everyone ought to ask. Do I hate evil and the sin in my life? Does the grace of faith lead to the grace of repentance?

The thought of the book of life being opened to measure the life and soul of a man or woman should dramatically affect that person's attitude toward the Judge before whom he or she will stand. Unfortunately many believe the final judgment will be a private conference with the Lord. At the judgment seat there are no private meetings, no special preferences, and no technicalities. That which was private in this life will become public. All grudges will be opened for all to see. All gossip will be exposed as lies. All slander will be vindicated publicly.

If professing Christians believe the Bible, they must believe in the judgment seat of Christ. If Christians believe there will be a judgment seat for all men, then it should affect their understanding of life and death. As the hymn writer put it "Nothing in my hand I bring, simply to the cross I cling."

The positive effect of the judgment seat of Christ is to believers what the negative effect is to unbelievers. It is the place God's children are given the reward of eternal life. Although Christians will stand before the judgment seat, they will not find condemnation or eternal punishment, but their works will be tested. It is abundantly clear from Scripture that the unbeliever stands condemned in the judgment. It is also abundantly clear that Christians are not condemned at the final judgment. Christians are forgiven, their works are tested and their ultimate reward is an eternal favorable relationship with God. This will be a righteous judgment, because Jesus Christ is a righteous judge.

The joy of the final judgment for Christians will be to stand before the righteous Judge who will say "Your sins are forgiven you..." (Luke 5:20-24). The eternal promise from God is that His second coming will be glorious. His final judgment will usher in His saints into that glorious eternal kingdom which is the great hope of all Christians.

The double effect theory applied to the second coming and final judgment has two very different effects on believers and unbelievers. His second coming and His final judgment will be a terror to those without Christ. However, His second coming and His final judgment will bring indescribable joy to those who believe. For the unbeliever the final words of the Lord Jesus Christ will be "I never knew you; depart from Me, you who practice lawlessness" (Matthew 7:23). For the believer, the final words of the Lord Jesus Christ will be "Well done, good and faithful servant; you have been faithful over a few things, I will make you ruler over many things. Enter into the joy of your lord" (Matthew 25:23).

Holy Spirit

What do Christians mean when they profess to believe in the Holy Spirit? First there are those professing Christians who believe the Holy Spirit is merely an impersonal being. The second group believes the Holy Spirit is so pro-active in the Christian life that He literally becomes a slave to the individual Christian. The third group believes the Holy Spirit is the third person of the Trinity, the eternal Spirit of God proceeding from the Father and the Son. The third group believes, as the *Westminster Shorter Catechism* explains, that the "Holy Spirit is the same in substance and equal in power and glory with God the Father and God the Son."

The inspired apostle Paul explains the divine nature of the Holy Spirit in His letter to the Corinthians. The Bible says, "the Lord is the Spirit" (2 Corinthians 3:17). When the Bible mentions the term "Holy Spirit" it is a reference to God. All the perfections of God are found in the Holy Spirit. The Holy Spirit is eternal and sovereign just as God the Father is eternal and sovereign.

It is not the design or purpose of this book to cover every aspect of the Holy Spirit, but there are three characteristics that belong to God the Father and God the Son that also belong to God the Holy Spirit.

The first characteristic is the power of the Holy Spirit. Just as God is all-powerful, so is the Holy Spirit all-powerful. An angel spoke to Mary before The birth of the Lord Jesus Christ and said "The Holy Spirit will come upon you, and the power of the Highest will overshadow you" (Luke 1:35). The power of the Holy Spirit is evident from the beginning of time. "The earth was without form, and void; and darkness was on the face of the deep. And the Spirit of God was hovering over the face of the waters" (Genesis 1:2). The power of the Holy Spirit is creative. The Holy Spirit not only has power to create material substance, it has the power to create and reform immaterial substance. Paul's letter to the Corinthians reads, "You are our epistle written in our hearts, known and read by all men; clearly you are an epistle of Christ, ministered by us, written not with ink but by the Spirit of the living God, not on tablets of stone, but on tablets of flesh, that is, of the heart" (2 Corinthians 3:2).

The human heart refers to the soul of man and the soul is sinful and corrupt. Man in his state of depravity, corrupt and sinful in every part of body and soul, not having any disposition to turn to God is given new life by the power of the Holy Spirit (2 Corinthians 3:6). It is the power of the Holy Spirit that brings new life to God's people. Without the power of the Holy Spirit changing the heart (the soul), sinners would plunge headlong into the hands of Satan and hell. With the power of the Holy Spirit changing the heart, sinners will turn to Christ in faith and repentance with a love for God never to be extinguished. The spiritual life of the soul takes a turn from darkness to light, from evil to good, from death to life by the power of the Holy Spirit. It is God the Holy Spirit that has the power to create and recreate the hearts of sinful men.

Another characteristic of the Holy Spirit is His knowledge. The Holy Spirit not only has knowledge, He knows everything. The combination of the Holy Spirit's power and knowledge has many good advantages for the Christian. The Holy Spirit knows all the needs of every individual Christian. He knows the mind is in need of illumination so the believer will understand what it means to be in a new relationship with God. That is precisely what John tells us in his inspired gospel. "But the Helper, the Holy Spirit, whom the Father will send in My name, He will teach you all things, and bring to your remembrance all things that I said to you" (John 14:26). What will He teach you? He will teach you the truth. "However, when He, the Spirit of truth, has come, He will guide you into all the truth" (John 16:13). When the Holy Spirit re-creates your mind you are open to understand divine knowledge. The knowledge given by the Holy Spirit is not merely some esoteric mystical spiritual knowledge; it is the rational intelligent understanding of truth. The truth of eternal life will be enlarged as the Holy Spirit empowers the new believer to read and understand the Word of God. The knowledge of truth has a sweet flavor. Truth is tasty and sweet to the rational mind. God gives it in great abundance to His adopted children.

Think of how precious and comforting it is to worship the Holy Spirit in truth. However, the truth about man, God, and existence is not merely abstract; truth ought to be the center of human expression and experience. The Holy Spirit knows that Christians need to know the truth, because they need to know reality. The opposite of reality is deception. Satan's whole purpose is to convince professing believers that God is not real. Satan wants to convince them that their relationship with God is not real. The primary objective in life is to know the saving truth of God and live by His sanctifying truth. The only way anyone can do that is for the Holy Spirit to guide them into all truth. The Holy Spirit is not only all-powerful and all knowing; He is everywhere present at once. "Where can I go from Your Spirit? Or where can I flee from Your presence? If I ascend into heaven, You are there: If I make my bed in Hell, behold, You are there (Psalm 139:7-8).

The work of the Holy Spirit can be found everywhere, even among unbelievers. The Bible manifestly teaches that the saving and sanctifying power of the Holy Spirit applies only to those who have been empowered to believe the gospel of God's saving grace. However the Holy Spirit works in a general sense among people everywhere. If the Holy Spirit restricted His activity only among believers, then the moral disposition of the world would be in utter chaos. Do you sometimes wonder why unbelievers act morally upright? It is because the Holy Spirit restricts the work of Satan in this world. Please note the following testimony from the mouth of the Lord Jesus Christ. "If the world hates you, you know that it has hated Me before it hated you. If you were of the world, the world would love its own. Yet because you are not of the world, but I chose you out of the world, therefore the world hates you" (John 15:18-19).

The context and the use of the word "world" refers to the evil and sinister beings who are associates of Satan. It was the world that crucified the Lord Jesus Christ. If the world hates you, why does it not kill you? What keeps the world from destroying you? It is the restraining power of the Holy Spirit. The Holy Spirit utilizes natural law and self interest as second causes to prevent utter destruction. It is because of the omnipresence (everywhere present at one time) of the Holy Spirit that the world is tame enough to live in.

The Holy Spirit demonstrates His power, knowledge and presence by giving Christians many gifts. By giving them the Word of God, He gives the words of life. Next to the enabling of the soul to believe, the gift of the Word of God is the great source of protection against the lies of Satan (Ephesians 6:17).

A military metaphor describes the relationship of the word of the Spirit and the work of the Spirit. The Bible says "take the helmet of salvation, and the sword of the Spirit, which is the Word of God" (Ephesians 6:17). The Holy Spirit gives Christians a heart to believe, and then He gives them His Word, the written and living Word, so they can understand His powerful work in overcoming all their enemies. Then the Holy Spirit gives Christians spiritual gifts to glorify God. The nature and character of the Holy Spirit demonstrated by His power, knowledge, and presence is a special comfort in this sinful life.

The saved sinner will find great delight in the presence and power of the Holy Spirit. Christians find comfort in His convicting power. The Holy Spirit loves the child of God and for that reason convicts them of their sins and brings them to compare themselves with the Law of God. When the comparison is made, a radical deficiency will be obvious. Then the saved sinner will see himself or herself contrary to the nature and character of God. It is the Holy Spirit that convinces them, not only of their sin, but also the threat of punishment and the misery that accompanies sin. Any estrangement from God is displeasing to the soul of a converted believer. It is the saving grace of God the Father through the work of God the Son by the power of the Holy Spirit that gives comfort and joy to the believing sinner's heart.

The Bible explicitly commands Christians to be filled with the Holy Spirit. "Do not be drunk with wine, in which is dissipation; but be filled with the Spirit" (Ephesians 5:18). There are two commandments, one negative and one positive: 1) do not be drunk and 2) be filled. A little more precision comes when the Greek text is consulted. The Greek text could literally be translated "be being filled." Even though it is a command it requires the work of the Holy Spirit to bring the commandment to its right place. A drunken person is out of his or her proper senses. The bodily functions including thinking, making decisions, and intelligent expressions are affected by drunkenness. The contrast to drunkenness is to be filled with the Holy Spirit. The Holy Spirit is able to bring sobriety and joy to life by filling the mind, will, and emotions with His peace.

The Holy Spirit is a person. You cannot have part of person or lose part of person. The Holy Spirit does not come and go. He does not diminish and fade away into the background. The primary operation of the Holy Spirit is to take up residence in the soul. The result is reconciliation and favor with God. Christians do not need more of the Holy Spirit, because He does not come in doses, but Christians ought to pray for the Holy Spirit to take over their lives and pray that every experience in life may be filled with the Holy Spirit. As the apostle said to the church at Corinth, "The Lord is the Spirit' (2 Corinthians 3:17) and "the Spirit gives life" (2 Corinthians 3:6). If the Holy Spirit has given you life, He will convict you of your sins. Then confess your sins, repent, ask forgiveness and endeavor to restore all broken relationships. Believe and live as one filled with the Spirit of God.

Holy Catholic Church

The church is the most significant institution in the history of the world. The church has influenced the progress and development of every country in the Western world. Why has the church become such an important and powerful institution? Is it because millions of people associate themselves with an institution commonly called the "church"?

Why do people go to church? Stanley High probably answered that question with astute reasoning that defines the meaning of "going to church" in the minds of most evangelicals in the United States. In the 1930's Stanley High was a writer and he wrote an article for the *Saturday Evening Post*. It was entitled "Why I Go to Church."

He gave 5 reasons:
1) He liked the preacher.
2) He found it convenient.
3) Habit compelled him.
4) It gave historical and moral perspective.
5) He got along better when he went to church.

Please think about the notion that Stanley High or any other person says, "I go to Church." It is an impossible notion. No one can go to church. Every Christian person constitutes the church so that the biblical meaning of the term "church" is a collective term for all those who belong to Jesus Christ. Christians do not go to church, but rather the church assembles to worship, teach or for some other biblical reason.

Stanley High attended a Presbyterian Church and many Presbyterians use the Apostles' Creed in their liturgy. So when Stanley High professed his faith he said, "I believe in the holy catholic church." His man-centered reason for attending church is inconsistent with the God-centered creed he professes. His reasons for attending were self-centered, while his creed was God-centered. Apparently he didn't understand three words: holy, catholic, and church.

The church of Jesus Christ is holy. The word holy in relation to the church means that the church would be set apart from all other institutions and organizations in the world. If the church is holy (set apart) the church would also consist of holy people (set apart). Holy is a synonym for saints. To be a member of the church means that one must be a saint. He or she is a saint not because of his or her ability or goodness, but because of the ability and goodness of Jesus Christ and His birth, life, suffering, death, burial, resurrection and intercession for the saints in the church. So it is that the church and the people in the church are holy because of the Lord Jesus Christ.

Secondly the church that Jesus Christ builds is catholic. The word "catholic" is traced to the Greek word *katholikos* which is translated universal. Our Lord explains that doctrine in the Gospel according to Matthew; "Go therefore and make disciples of all the nations, baptizing them in the name of the Father and the Son and the Holy Spirit" (Matthew 28:19). The true church has no boundaries thus it is not parochial, but rather it is evangelical.

The church is holy and the church is universal, but what is the nature of the church? There is not a specific proof text that defines the nature of the church. A careful and diligent study of the full counsel of God reveals that the nature of the church is expressed in Scripture within two dimensions.

The church militant is the visible church.
The church triumphant is the invisible church.

The church visible is mixed with wheat and tares (See 2 Timothy 2:14-19). One church creed describes the visible church as the whole "number of professing Christians, with their children, associated together for divine worship and godly living, agreeable to the Scriptures and submitting to the lawful government of Christ's kingdom" (*Westminster Confession of Faith*, chapter 25, section 1). Notice that confession refers to professing Christians. There may be a difference in professing Christians and actual Christians.

The church invisible is the church in heaven. The invisible church is the true church or to put it another way the saved church. The invisible church is:

Infallible; It is exempt from error.
Indestructible; cannot be separated from God.
Indivisible; see John 17 "that they may be one."
Universal; includes every nation and every tongue.

The theological basis for the nature of the church is best understood by the concepts known as the visible and invisible church.

The metaphors in the Bible describe the nature of the church. A metaphor refers to the likeness between two different objects or ideas. For example, Jesus said "I have other sheep" (John 10:16). Jesus used the word sheep referring to His disciples in a culture that thought of sheep as four legged animals. In the context of John's gospel, Jesus used the word sheep to refer to His disciples. Jesus used several metaphors to explain and define the nature of the church.

One prominent metaphor used in the Bible is the vineyard. Jesus told the parable of the land owner that planted a vineyard. He made arrangements with share croppers to work the vineyard. Both the owner and the workers would share in the profits. The workers decided not to give the owner his share. The owner decided to destroy the wicked workers and give the vineyard to other workers. Jesus addressed this parable to the chief priests and elders of Israel, the church of the Old Testament. After Jesus finished the parable He said, "the kingdom of God will be taken from you and given to a nation bearing the fruits of it" (Matthew 21:43). From the words of Jesus we find the nature of the vineyard is productivity. So it is with the church. The church is productive when it fulfills the responsibilities given to the church by the Head and King of the church, the Lord Jesus Christ.

The Bible assigns the church the responsibility for making disciples, not an outside organization such as parachurch organizations. The church is responsible for teaching the full counsel of God, not any other organization. The church is responsible for worship, orderly government, and redemptive discipline. Of course every individual Christian must engage in the purpose, mission, and ministry of the church.

Another metaphor that defines the nature of the church is the field. Paul said to the Corinthian Church: "we are God's fellow workers; you are God's field" (1 Corinthians 3:9). The emphasis on the field is ownership. The field belongs to God; therefore the church belongs to God. Too often I hear Christians talk like they own the church with comments like "my church."

They do not understand the nature of the church. The church belongs to God.

Another agricultural metaphor in the Bible describes the nature of the church. The metaphor found often in the gospel of John is a flock. Raising sheep was common in all ancient Near Eastern cultures. Sheep provided food, clothing, and sacrifices for religious worship. Jesus said "the sheep hear his voice; and he calls his own sheep by name and leads them out" (John 10:3). The sheep need a shepherd to tend to them and protect them. So the elders of the church are the appointed means by God to tend to the sheep and protect them.

One of my favorite metaphors used to describe the nature of the church is the family of God. The biblical concept of the family calls for order, harmony, and unity. The modern notion that families are normal even when the various parties are disaffected is the very reason that churches feud, fight, and divide. If children in the family do not agree and live in unity, neither can siblings in the family of God get along. The nature of the church is such that order, harmony, and unity are necessary for the church to demonstrate its unique character.

The body is a metaphor that stresses the unity of the church. The body is the most prominent image of the church in the writings of the apostle Paul. The Bible explains that the church is "one body" therefore unity is a mark of the church. Unity does not violate the individual gifts of individual members. There is a diversity of gifts because the Bible says the church consists of many members (1 Corinthians 12:13). The goal of the church is to grow up into Him who is the Head, that is Christ (Ephesians 4:15).

The Bible also describes the church as a bride. The Biblical bride is supposed to be pure, and so it is with the church. The biblical bride submits to, honors, and obeys the groom, the Lord Jesus Christ. The nature of the church is such that man and God are inseparably connected.

Given the biblical teachings on the nature of the church what does Jesus mean when He said "I will build my church?" Does the Lord mean that He would build a building? The inspired apostle Paul says no! "And what agreement has the temple of God with idols? For you are the temple of the living God. As God has said: I will dwell in them and walk among them. I will be their God and they shall be My people" (2 Corinthians. 6:16).

Many if not most professing Christians think of the church in terms of a physical piece of architecture. The place or building where professing Christians assemble for worship, Bible study, and fellowship has become a synonym for the church. I cannot begin to describe how much suffering has accompanied the terrible mistake of calling the building where Christians assemble for worship, instruction, and fellowship, a church. Is the building where the name of the church appears on a sign or a marquee the church? The place where Christians assemble for worship or Bible study is not a church. The church is a spiritual building, built by God. The church in biblical terms is not a building made by men, but rather a building created in the image of God. The Holy Spirit resides in the building called the church. "Living stones" is the description given by Peter for those who form and shape God's building (See 1 Peter 2:5). This must mean that God's building consists of the souls of Christians filled with the Holy Spirit of God.

The inspired words of the apostle Paul in his letter to Timothy says, " I write so that you may know how one ought to conduct himself in the household of God, which is the church of the living God, the pillar and support of the truth" (1 Timothy. 3:15). Truth and nothing but the truth is acceptable in God's building. Falsehood and lies are not acceptable. The church is supposed to be the place to find truth; the truth about God, the truth about man, the truth about how to live, the truth about eternity, and all the truth from the Word of God.

If the church is the place to find truth, Christians must have a true understanding of the church rather than a false understanding of the church. Unfortunately the church has traditionally served as the center of social and cultural functions, thus associating the church with a building. It was the building that provided entertainment to the body rather than enrichment to the soul. Many have sadly adopted the view that a church is nothing more than a building and a membership roll.

It is difficult to set aside old habits and tradition passed on from previous generations. Even so, I hope you will reconsider the nature of the church and re-examine what the Bible has to say about the church. The nature of the church is inseparably connected with the nature of Jesus Christ. To ignore the true biblical teaching on the nature of the church is to ignore Jesus Christ.

The nature of the church defines the "isness" or the essence of the church. The church also has a purpose, mission, and ministry.

Let me quote a theologian who was ahead of his time.

The church has almost dwindled down into a secular corporation; and the principles of this world, a mere carnal policy, which we have nick-named prudence, presides in our councils. Until she becomes a spiritual body, and aims at spiritual ends by appointed means, and makes faith in God the impulsive cause of her efforts, our Zion can never arise and shine, and become a joy and a praise in the whole earth. (James H. Thornwell, February 7, 1842)

One substantial abuse the church has suffered since the time Thornwell wrote "The church has almost dwindled down into a secular corporation" is the misunderstanding of the first and primary purpose of the church. The primary purpose of the church is to worship the triune God. The primary purpose of the church is to gather with other like-minded believers and offer worship to God (John 4:24; Revelation 14:1-3).

The Old Testament types and stories give a vivid picture of the congregation "coming to worship." My favorite narrative text is found in the book of Jeremiah. "Thus says the Lord: 'Stand in the court of the Lord's house, and speak to all the cities of Judah, which come to worship in the Lord's house, all the words that I command you to speak to them. Do not diminish a word'" (Jeremiah 26:2). This text from Jeremiah records a scene in the life of the Old Testament church that occurred about 2600 years ago. The one thing that the contemporary church has in common with the church of 2600 years ago is worship.

The people of God in the day of Jehoiakim the king of Judah (609-597) came to the Lord's house to worship. When the people gathered to worship, God warned the worshipers: "I will make this house like

Shiloh" unless the people turn from their evil ways. The worshipers could not entertain the thought of terminating worship at Jerusalem. The worshipers were outraged and threatened to kill the preacher.

Why did they get mad at the preacher? Apparently because Jeremiah said, speaking for God of course, "I (God) will make this house like Shiloh." Why was Shiloh so important? Shiloh became a place of worship for the Old Testament worshipers during the conquest under the direction of Joshua some 850 years before the scene in Jeremiah. Shiloh was the place of worship under the priesthood of Eli and his two wicked sons. After the Philistines captured the Ark of the Lord, Shiloh lost its significance and was eventually destroyed about 1050 B. C.

When Jeremiah said "this place" (the temple in Jerusalem), the place where the worshipers were presently standing will be like Shiloh, the worshipers were real upset. The preacher was tampering with their church and their worship. Attitudes toward worship have not changed much in the past 2600 years. Today the murmuring might be something like "What do you mean tampering with my church! I was baptized here and I love this building."

Many churches at the beginning of the 21st century have replaced true worship with entertainment of every sort. The application of managerial theory and psychobabble are the great enemies of true biblical worship. Today as in the day of Jeremiah, the focus is on the worshiper rather than the object of worship. It seems to me that professing Christian worshipers seem more interested in entertainment for themselves rather than worshiping the Creator.

By now someone may ask "what about evangelism, Christian fellowship, and Christian growth?" God in His wisdom gave the church a mission and ministry so He would be glorified and His people might worship Him. The mission of the church is apostolic. The ministry includes the works of service necessary for the mission.

The Latin word *missio*, from which we get the English word mission, refers to "a sending forth." The Greek word *apostello*, from which we get the word apostle, refers to "one sent by authority of the sender to act on the senders behalf." The gospels and the Acts of the Apostles' magnify the apostolic mission of the church (Matthew 28:18-20; John 17:6-18; Acts 13:1-3). The Lord Jesus Christ was sent on a mission and He sends every Christian (His disciples that constitute the church) on a mission. The two dimensions of the mission given by injunction are to make disciples and to teach holiness.

Evangelism is part of the process necessary to make disciples. However, instruction for the purpose of conversion is only one aspect of making disciples. Discipleship is an educational process. Every Christian is a disciple. A Christian disciple is simply someone who learns from a teacher. A disciple is one who learns, believes, and practices the truth. Preaching the whole counsel of God is necessary for the convert to become a disciple. Christians are students of Jesus Christ by God's appointed means. The two primary instruments include a curriculum and a teacher. The Bible is the curriculum and ordained elders of the church are the teachers.

Ministry is the spiritual and physical labor of every person that belongs to the body of Christ. The authority for ministry has been given to the church through men called to prepare God's people for works of service (Ephesians 4:11-16). Christ has given elders to the church so every member in the body would be prepared to serve according to the gifts distributed by the Holy Spirit.

Every Christian should be involved in the ministry of the church according to the gift that Christ has given to every individual Christian. The ministry of the church depends on the unity of the faith, full knowledge of Jesus, and spiritual maturity. A spiritually mature man in contrast to a child "tossed to and fro with every wind of doctrine" is necessary for the effective ministry of the body of Christ.

The Bible explains the nature, purpose, mission, and ministry of the church. The people of God ought to embrace this doctrine and teach this doctrine so that the church will "become a joy and praise in the whole earth"

The challenge to every congregation of God's people is to admit that the church has been abused, used, and amused through the centuries. Every congregation of God's people everywhere in the world ought to be honest with the creedal statement that says "I believe in the holy catholic church." It will take diligent study and real effort to set aside the traditional views of the church and adopt the dynamic views as they are found in the Word of God.

Communion of the Saints

When Christians announce the Apostles' Creed as a profession of faith, there is a basic assumption. They believe what they say. Furthermore, they believe that each doctrinal statement logically and theologically leads to the next doctrine in the creed.

For example, the doctrine of the universality of the church precedes the doctrine of the communion of the saints. The Bible declares that the redeemed people of God make up the universal Church. The redeemed universal church will remain strong only if it follows the principles given by God to His people. The affirmation "I believe in the communion of the saints" is a biblical principle, which must put into practice in the universal church.

The communion of the saints was one of the distinguishing marks of the early church. The word communion literally means fellowship. The Greek word *koinonia* means to have a share in something or to participate in something. To put it another way fellowship is a condition because two or more people have something in common.

The communion of saints is the fellowship of the saints. The apostle John wrote a letter to the early church because of disruption in the fellowship. The traditional view is that the apostle John wrote his letter after the church had spread over much of the Middle East. In fact, John mentions the estrangement. "They went out from us, but they were not of us; for if they had been of us, they would have continued with us; but they went out, in order that it might be made manifest, that none of them were of us" (1 John 2:19). If there is no unity, there is no fellowship. The emphasis in the opening words of John's letter is the unity of the church. "That which was from the beginning, which we have heard, which we have seen with our eyes, which we have looked upon, and our hands have handled, concerning the word of life-the life was manifested, and we have seen, and bear witness and declare to you...that you also may have fellowship with us...(1 John 1:1-3). Perhaps a simple paradigm will help us understand those verses.

> We have heard.
> We have seen with our eyes.
> We have looked upon.
> We bear witness.
> We declare to you.
> "We" refers to the church.
> Therefore, we may have fellowship.

The members of the early church had heard, seen, witnessed, and declared the Word of life. John intended to show the church then and the church today that believers must have a common belief in the truth of Christianity and the common belief "we" equals the church is necessary for communion with each other. If this sounds like an appeal for unity among believers, that is true. It is a biblical commandment to have communion with one another; therefore there must be some common agreement on the doctrine of Scripture. Paul understood that fellowship among believers is in response to the Word of God. Paul explained to the Philippian church that "if there is any fellowship of the Spirit fulfill my joy by being like-minded" (Philippians 2:2). The church ought to desire and maintain brotherly fellowship with the children of God according to the commandments found in Scripture.

If there is no like-mindedness there will not be much fellowship. The prophet Amos said, "Do two men walk together unless they are agreed?" (Amos 3:3). The text in Amos is relative to the dynamic known as doctrinal fellowship. The New Testament church at its very beginning in Jerusalem understood the connection between doctrinal unity and fellowship of the saints. The connection may be seen in the inspired normative history of Scripture revealed during the early days of the New Testament church. "And they were continually devoting themselves to the apostles' teaching and to fellowship, to the breaking of bread and to prayer" (Acts 2:42). Obviously doctrine and fellowship went together like hand and glove. It is the mutual agreement to the Word of God that brings fellowship to its full meaning. The concept of fellowship becomes invalid without common agreement. It is the common agreement with the Word of God that makes the church collectively unified. So by necessity fellowship is collective, not individual. The church is a collective body of godly believers who form a religious community, which the Apostles' Creed calls a fellowship.

Before Christians have a right relationship with one another, they have to be in a right relationship with Jesus Christ. "God is faithful, by whom you were called into the fellowship of His Son, Jesus Christ our Lord" (1 Corinthians 1:9). "Therefore if there is any consolation in Christ, if there is any comfort of love, if any fellowship of the Spirit, if any affection and mercy, fulfill my joy by being like-minded" (Philippians 2:1-2). If professing believers are not rightly connected with Jesus Christ, they have no communion in the church of Jesus Christ. If they are rightly connected with Jesus Christ, then believers have a unique relationship with other Christians. Based on evidence and my personal observation there has either been a misunderstanding of the communion of saints or a failure to live up to the oft quoted creed, "I believe in the communion of saints." Scripture teaches and the creed affirms that the type of communion or fellowship Christians have with fellow believers is the sharing of a common life together. The general principle taught in Scripture is that Christians are one in Christ Jesus. Even though there is only one vine, there are many branches. Although there is only one family, there are many children. Even though there is only one Christ, His life flows through the lives of all those who belong to Him. When Christians practice fellowship with each other it reflects their relationship with Christ.

Fellowship with Christ translates into vital personal spiritual growth and good health for the church. Unfortunately Christians have become so desensitized and depersonalized by technology and modern communication that they have little fellowship with other Christians. They are trained by the modern techniques of tracking people rather than knowing people. Try to conduct a business transaction without a social security number. Try to cash a check without a drivers license number. We are known by our social security number, our driver's license number or our zip code. In this depersonalized world of automation and computerization, there is great need for fellowship.

It must be taught in every Christian church; Christians are commanded in Scripture to have fellowship with each other. There are reciprocal commands in Scripture that reveal the true nature of biblical fellowship. Commandments such as forgive one another, love one another, bear one another burdens, pray for one another, encourage one another, teach one another, honor one another, are reciprocal commandments that bring the communion of saints into proper perspective. Christians may know those commandments, but do they know what they mean and how to apply them to the concept of Christian fellowship? How can Christians agree to love one another if they neglect the biblical doctrine of love? How can Christians forgive one another if they fail to understand the biblical doctrine of forgiveness? For example, there is a huge division in the church over the doctrine of forgiveness and reconciliation. There must be like-mindedness on the doctrine of forgiveness and reconciliation in order to have mutual fellowship. I will write more about the "one another" commandments in chapter twenty one.

The modern church recognized the failure to bring its members into true fellowship and came up with a solution. Build fellowship halls onto what is commonly called the church. The only way to practice Christian fellowship with those who hold the biblical doctrine in contradiction is to redefine the meaning of Christian fellowship or eliminate any doctrinal discussion. The way to eliminate the discussion of biblical doctrine was to build fellowship halls. When Christians meet in the fellowship hall they can talk about superficial mundane subjects relative to work, politics, sports, entertainment, leisure, any form of gossip or anything else, but no discussions about biblical doctrine. If they discuss biblical doctrine there might be some disagreement and that would break up the fellowship meeting. Fellowship halls have not produced true communion among the community of believers. The challenge for churches everywhere is to understand that fellowship is the sharing of a common life together based on the Word of God. The emphasis is not on the individual Christian, but rather on the community of believers.

Christian fellowship is not merely common agreement with the doctrine of Scripture. Christian fellowship is also a matter of duty and responsibility. "But whoever has the world's goods, and beholds his brother in need and closes his heart against him, how does the love of God abide in him? My little children, let us not love with word or with tongue, but in deed and truth" (1 John 3:17, 18). The inspired apostle is not talking about communism. Christian communion is not the same thing as communism. The inspired account of Ananias and Sapphira in the early church is sufficient evidence that the Bible does not teach any form of communism.

> But a certain man named Ananias, with his wife Sapphira, sold a piece of property, and kept back some of the price for himself, with his wife's full knowledge, and bringing a portion of it, he laid it at the apostles' feet. But Peter said, "Ananias, why has Satan filled your heart to lie to the Holy Spirit, and to keep back some of the price of the land? While it remained unsold, did it not remain your own? And after it was sold, was it not under your control? Why is it that you have conceived this deed in your heart? You have not lied to men, but to God. And as he heard these words, Ananias fell down and breathed his last; and great fear came upon all who heard of it. Peter said, "While it remained was it not your own. While it remained was it not in your power to do what you would with it. (Acts 5:1-5)

Neither the church nor the leaders of the church demanded any money. It belonged to Ananias and Sapphira until they pledged it and lied about it.

Communism teaches that all property belongs to the state. Communism says, "I will take what you have and I will distribute it according to my best judgment." Christian fellowship, on the other hand, teaches that each one gives according to God's generous providence. Christians give because of what Christ has given them.

Christ poured out His life and His blood so that your union with Him would lead to fellowship with others of like precious faith. The biblical doctrine on fellowship reveals the spiritual condition of the individual in relation to others in the body of Christ. The lack of true fellowship may be a sign of spiritual deprivation. Maybe the doctrine of the communion of the saints has overwhelmed you? It should in light of the condition of the universal church in the 21st century.

The fellowship of the saints in the church depends on the spiritual condition of the individual members of the church. If there are wicked, evil, envious, greedy and heretical people in the church, the spiritual condition of the church is in decline and must be restored. The Bible warns Christians not to have fellowship in the unfruitful deeds of darkness (Ephesians 5:11). If the members of the church are filled with love, joy, peace, kindness, and goodness then the church will demonstrate true fellowship and secure the prosperity of the church by the communion of saints.

Forgiveness of Sins

It may sound odd that the Apostles' Creed teaches the doctrine of the forgiveness of sins. It should sound odd because the creed never mentions anything about the sinful condition of the human race. The creed does not have a chapter on sin and there is a good reason for it. The first and great need for Christians is to understand the nature and character of God and then the nature and character of man's sinfulness will be manifestly evident. Although the Apostles' Creed does not make a statement about the sinful condition of man, it does go into great detail about the sacrificial work of Christ which would not be necessary without the condition known as sin. Apparently those who formed the creed assumed everyone understood the doctrine of sin. The Bible has plenty to say about sin. The individual Christian says, "Behold, I was brought forth in iniquity, and in sin my mother conceived me" (Psalm 51:5). The Bible also speaks to the entire human race. "The wicked are estranged from the womb; They go astray as soon as they are born, speaking lies" (Psalm 58:3). The Bible leaves no doubt, "For all have sinned and fall short of the glory of God" (Romans 3:23).The Bible declares that all people including believers are sinners.

The Bible also defines sin. Under inspiration from God the apostle John defined sin. "Whoever commits sin also commits lawlessness, and sin is lawlessness" (1 John 3:4). People sin by breaking the law of God. They sin when they deviate from God's objective standards. They sin by rebelling against God. They sin by missing the mark of God's perfect standard. "For whoever shall keep the whole law and yet stumble in one point he is guilty of all" (James 2:10). James must mean that the least sin is a sin against the law Maker who gave the whole law. That means everyone disobeys God. Therefore, sin is the omission of what God has commanded or sin is doing something that God has forbidden. How do Christians know what God has commanded or forbidden? For unbelievers it is found in natural law (Romans 2:14, 15) and for Christians it is found in the Word of God (Exodus 20:1-17).

What happens when someone sins? The answer is simple in one sense and profound in another. Sin causes guilt. The 17th century scholar Francis Turretin gives a clear and brief, but definitive statement on guilt. Turretin said, "Guilt is the obligation to punishment from previous sin" (*Institutes of Elenctic Theology*, by Francis Turretin, vol. 1, p. 594). Adam's sin was sufficient to require the condemnation of the entire human race. My understanding of the Word of God is that guilt is the liability to punishment for wrongdoing. I know people have told me that guilt is an internal feeling based on an emotional hunch. Guilt does affect the emotions, but guilt also affects the whole person, the mind, will, and emotions. It is the guilt of sin that causes distress and discontentment to the soul. So, how is the guilt removed? Guilt is removed by confession, repentance, forgiveness and reconciliation. If the guilt is not removed the result will be a hard and impenitent heart and finally God's wrath. The Book of Romans explains the doctrine of un-removed guilt. "For the wrath of God is revealed from heaven against all ungodliness and unrighteousness of men, who suppress the truth in unrighteousness" (Romans 1:18). Then the Bible explains what happens when guilt remains. "And he [Zedekiah] also rebelled against King Nebuchadnezzar who had made him swear an oath by God; but he [Zedekiah] stiffened his neck and hardened his heart against turning to the Lord God of Israel" (2 Chronicles 36:13). The expression "he stiffened his neck" refers to his stubborn rebellious attitude towards God's providential wrath poured out because of Judah's sin. Zedekiah refused to confess, repent, and ask forgiveness. Zedekiah went further by hardening his heart against God. Zedekiah's guilt was not removed. The punishment was terrible. His sons were killed before his eyes, then his eyes were put out, and he was tied in chains and taken as a slave to Babylon. In the end, the horror of God's punishment will fall upon those who are guilty before Him. The logical summary is:

> All men are sinners.
> All men are guilty.
> All guilty men deserve due punishment.
> Therefore, all men need forgiveness of that guilt.

Someone must pay the penalty for breaking God's law so God can grant forgiveness. What is the penalty for breaking God's law? The answer is death. Then is there any hope? Is there any forgiveness? Yes, through the shed blood of the Lord Jesus Christ who paid the penalty of death for those who believe and trust Him for eternal life. "In Him we have redemption through His blood, the forgiveness of our sins, according to the riches of His grace" (Ephesians. 1:7). When the guilt is removed the forgiven sinner will find peace, joy, hope, and life eternal in God's glorious favorable presence. Martin Luther said the "forgiveness of sins through Christ is the highest article of our faith." The reason Luther said that is because of his understanding of God's holiness and man's sinful heart.

Sin is like a wall between God and man. Sin severs the favorable relationship between God and man. The only remedy for that separation is forgiveness. An understanding of forgiveness from God's perspective will help Christians understand their responsibility to practice the doctrine of forgiveness. Just as sin sets up a wall or barrier between God and man, sin also sets up a barrier between people. Therefore, the doctrine of mutual forgiveness becomes a nemesis or joy for the individual Christian.

The only way to know how to forgive one another is to model our forgiveness after God's forgiveness. The Word of God tells the Christian to "be kind to one another, tenderhearted, forgiving one another, even as God in Christ forgave you" (Ephesians 4:32). Notice the manner in which God forgives. "I will forgive their iniquity, and their sin I will remember no more" (Jeremiah 31:34). This text does not mean that God is forgetful, but after God forgives, He does not bring up the sin again. God is omniscient. He cannot forget anything, but He simply does not bring the imputed sin of Adam or the actual sins into account after He forgives. "As far as the east is from the west, so far has He removed our transgressions from us" (Psalm. 103:12). How a Christian feels about sin and forgiveness does not determine the reality of forgiveness. What counts is objective reality which is found in the Word of God. Christians must judge according to truth, not how they feel about truth. God doesn't forgive because He feels like it. God forgives because of His grace and mercy.

Does anyone deserve forgiveness? The Bible answers the question with a rhetorical question that every person ought to ask. "If You, Lord, should mark iniquities, O Lord, who could stand?" (Psalm. 130:3).

God, by His pure grace, forgives you of your multiplied sins against Him. When Christians say "we believe in the forgiveness of sins" they believe they have been forgiven of the thousands upon thousands of sins that have been removed by the sacrifice of the Lord Jesus Christ. Then likewise, by grace, Christians forgive each other. In His model prayer Jesus instructs His people to call upon God and ask for forgiveness of sins (Luke 11:1-4). I have never personally heard of a Christian refusing to ask God for forgiveness of sins. However, it is a common habit for Christians to refuse to ask one another for forgiveness. In the Lord's model prayer Christians are instructed to ask God to forgive their sins and to forgive everyone who is indebted to them. The purpose, mission, and ministry of the church will be stigmatized because Christians who have offended and sinned against other Christians have not asked for forgiveness, which means a debt remains unpaid. The word "debt" is important. This portion of the prayer means that when one Christian sins against another Christian, the offending party has an obligation to the offended party or to put it another way, that person has a debt to pay. This "debt" does not refer to a financial transaction between Christians. It does not mean that God's forgiveness may be earned by forgiving a brother or sister in Christ. If Christians practice or refuse to practice the biblical doctrine of forgiveness, it is evidence of a spiritual condition.

When the Bible commands Christians to "forgive one another" the necessity and emphasis is on mutual forgiveness. The doctrine is very clear. God, by His pure grace, forgives the sinner of his or her multiplied sins against God, and then the forgiven sinner must forgive others who sin against him or her. When Christians forgive, truly forgive, they are simply following the example of the Lord and give evidence of the grace of the Lord Jesus Christ present in the soul. If you are not able to forgive others who have offended you and sinned against you, then you have not received any forgiveness from God. This is hard doctrine for many professing Christians to accept, but the Word of God is very clear. Listen to the words that come directly from the mouth of the Lord Jesus Christ. "For if you forgive men their trespasses, your heavenly Father will also forgive you. But if you do not forgive men their trespasses, neither will your Father forgive your trespasses" (Matthew 6:14, 15). First the Lord addresses it positively: "For if you forgive men their trespasses, your heavenly Father will also forgive you." Then the Lord addresses it negatively: "But if you do not forgive men their trespasses, neither will your Father forgive your trespasses." This does not mean that God's forgiveness is contingent upon you forgiving another person. It does mean that you will be compelled to forgive the other person if God has forgiven you. To forgive the other person means to remove from your mind any wrath, hatred, or desire for revenge. To forgive means to willingly, gladly, generously, and finally forget any injustice you may have experienced in your relationship with the other person. The Word of God is so clear and so loud I do not understand how Christians can misread it or misinterpret it, or misunderstand it. Christians must forgive the way God forgives. Forgiveness must come from the heart. Forgiveness comes from the depth of the soul involving the mind, will, and emotions.

Jesus told the parable of the unforgiving servant. It is the story of one person that was forgiven a large debt, but that same man refused to forgive someone else a much smaller debt (Matthew 18:21-35). The conclusion to the parable should be thought provoking. "So My heavenly Father also will do to you if each of you, from his heart, does not forgive his brother his trespasses" (Matthew 18:35). The warnings in Scripture should cause every believer to search the heart to know what to do. "These are the things you shall do: Speak each man the truth to his neighbor; Give judgment in your gates for truth, justice, and peace; Let none of you think evil in your heart against your neighbor; And do not love a false oath. For all these are things that I hate says the Lord" (Zechariah 8:16, 17). There are other factors that are relative to the biblical doctrine of forgiveness. Like any other teaching in Scripture, the whole counsel of God must come under scrutiny. For instance confession, repentance, and reconciliation are all connected with forgiveness.

God commands confession for forgiveness. Confess means you acknowledge the sin and agree with your brother that it is sin (1 John 1:9; James 5:16; Matthew 18:15).

Repentance is necessary if the confession is sincere and true; "Take heed to yourselves. If your brother sins against you, rebuke him; and if he repents, forgive him" (Luke 17:3).

Reconciliation is just as important as repentance. Forgiveness means that the sin will never be brought up again and the relationship is restored (Matthew 5:24; 2 Corinthians 5:18-19; Psalm 103:12).

Too often Christians dismiss the doctrine of reconciliation. I have heard professing Christians say, "I'll forgive, but I will not be reconciled." The Bible makes it clear that reconciliation is an essential part of forgiveness. To deny the doctrine of reconciliation would be like God saying, "I'll forgive you, but I do not want to ever see you again." The Bible speaks of reconciliation before the judgment day (Matthew 5:21-26). This text is for the occasion when you remember that your Christian brother believes you have sinned against him. It is one of the most difficult sayings of the Lord Jesus Christ: "You will by no means get out of there" (Matthew 5:26). This certainly implies that two Christian believers are in a broken relationship because of sin. Everything possible should be done to resolve the broken relationship so the two parties may be reconciled. If one person refuses to forgive, then the guilt will rest upon the person who refused to forgive. This is so important and may sound strange, but study the Word of God carefully. God promises to forgive, but woe to the person who refuses to forgive and be reconciled.

Reconciliation means peace. Do you want peace with God and peace with other Christians? If the answer is yes, I urge you to remember the words of the Psalmist. "I acknowledged my sin to Thee, And my iniquity I did not hide; I said, 'I will confess my transgressions to the Lord'; And Thou didst forgive the guilt of my sin" (Psalm 32:5).

The one word I want and I hope you want written on your headstone is: Forgiven.

Resurrection of the Body

The resurrection of the body is the great promise of the Christian religion. Those who do not believe in the resurrection of the body have a long history in western civilization. The Greek Epicureans denied the resurrection of the dead 400 years before the birth of Christ. The Roman writer, Pliny, called the resurrection "childish nonsense" (*Institutes of Elenctic Theology*, by Francis Turretin, vol. 3, p. 562). Professing believers under the old covenant as well as the new covenant have denied the resurrection of the body. The Bible reveals that during Paul's visit to Athens the Athenians mocked Paul when they heard of the resurrection of the dead.

The party of the Sadducees was a Jewish sect during the Lord's earthly life. Although it is said that they were more political than religious, it cannot be denied that they were closely connected with the priesthood and temple in Jerusalem. Sadducees, figuratively speaking, were prominent church leaders. As to their doctrine, they denied the immortality of the soul and the resurrection of the dead.

Before we condemn the Sadducees too quickly, we should remember the history of the church. Various alleged Christians through the centuries have denied the resurrection of the body. So should we be surprised when the liberal Jewish leaders expressed disdain for the mystery of the resurrection. About 600 years before the Sadducees came on the scene we find this stunning report: "Let us eat and drink, for tomorrow we die" (Isaiah 22:13). Even some professing believers think that death is the end of existence. Some Christian cults and several mainline theologians have repudiated the doctrine of eternal punishment. So why not "eat and drink, for tomorrow we die?" The unbeliever understands that the resurrection means an eternity of suffering so the solution for the unbeliever is to deny it.

Even the remaining corruption of sin causes believers to bring to question the hope of the resurrection. The Corinthian believers in the New Testament questioned the resurrection. "Now if Christ is preached that He has been raised from the dead, how do some among you say that there is no resurrection of the dead?" (1 Corinthians 15:12). Today there are many who profess the Christian religion and yet they either outright deny the resurrection of the dead or at least question it. They do not see any remedy for death, because dead men do not come back from the grave. The mystery of the resurrection must not be held in contempt. The resurrection is a mystery only in the sense that God has chosen not to reveal every detail of His filial and full power.

It is sufficient that God's Word, both written and living, is the ultimate source of our hope and confidence. His Word plainly teaches that by virtue of God's grace, those who belong to Jesus Christ are worthy to share in the resurrection. The operative words are "those who belong to Jesus Christ." Only those, who are called God's people, actually hold the resurrection of the body close to their souls, because they believe the promises of God. God's people during the Old Testament, New Testament, and throughout Church history have believed in the resurrection. The Lord Jesus Christ specifically mentions Moses and burning bush (Luke 20:37). There are numerous references in the Bible to the resurrection of the dead. It is widely held that Job is one of the oldest books in the Bible and Job believed in the resurrection of the dead. "For I know that my Redeemer lives, And He shall stand at last on the earth. And after my skin is destroyed, this I know, That in my flesh I shall see God" (Job 19:25-26).

Job was confident of the future resurrection, not only of His Redeemer, the Lord Jesus Christ, but also in the resurrection of the dead. Notice Job said, "Yet from my flesh I shall see God." Job speaks of seeing God in his resurrection body with real eyes. Later Jesus would say "blessed are the pure in heart, for they shall see God" (Matthew 5:8).

The apostle Paul said, "For now we see in a mirror dimly, but then face to face" (1 Corinthians 13:12). All of God's people want to see God, and if Job and Paul are right, they want to see him from the eyes of a resurrection body. There is one other verse worthy of attention. "Beloved, now we are children of God; and it has not yet been revealed what we shall be, but we know that when He is revealed, we shall be like Him, for we shall see Him as He is" (1 John 3:2). Notice John says "we shall be like Him." His resurrection proves that there is a higher principle than death. It is life in the resurrection body. The evidence from Scripture and historical sources for His resurrection leaves no question that it actually happened. It has been said that there is more evidence that Jesus Christ rose from the dead than it is that Julius Caesar was a real person.

The biblical doctrine relative to the resurrection body teaches that the resurrection body will be like the risen Christ (See 1 Corinthians 15:49; Philippians 3:21). Scripture does give an idea of what the resurrection body will be like. The first and the most important aspect of the resurrection body is that it never dies. Jesus told the Sadducees that in this life people marry.

God's covenant in the beginning was "be fruitful and multiply" because without marriage the human race would cease to exist. In the resurrection there is no need for marriage, because there is no death.

The resurrection body is synonymous with life. It is not just life, but life in the likeness of Jesus Christ. The wonderful promise from Scripture is "we have borne the image of the man of dust, we shall also bear the image of the heavenly Man" (1 Corinthians 15:49). The Word of God reveals, by comparison, the present state of our earthly bodies in relation to the future state of our resurrection bodies (1 Corinthians 15:42-47).

There are differences between the earthly body and the resurrection body. Earthly bodies, which Paul describes, are natural. They are made of dust. That means the body was made from the natural elements of this world. Since the natural elements are under the curse of sin, eventually the effect of sin will cause the body to die, decay and return to dust. Paul goes on to say that earthly bodies are dishonorable. The power of sin brought about a sense of humiliation. Earthly bodies are not only the subjects of humiliation they are the subjects of weakness. The weakness of the body is evident from birth to death. The most powerless thing on earth is a corpse. It is absolutely powerless. It cannot do anything except decay and return to dust.

The resurrection body, which is characterized by its spiritual nature, but nevertheless a real body, is a body that will never die and will no longer suffer humiliation. The resurrection body will be a glorious body accompanied by spiritual power. There is a tendency to try to hold on to natural human strength, especially as the years go by. Children and young people have energy to spare, but as people grow older, their bodies lose that energy. I've often heard the expression; "I can hardly drag myself out of bed." The resurrection body will never get tired. Scripture says the resurrection body will have no need for sleep. What a glorious and magnificent body God will provide on the resurrection day.

The confidence for the resurrection of the body is based on the evidence and reality of the resurrection of the Lord Jesus Christ. For Christians it is undeniable that Jesus Christ rose from the dead, has a real body and is waiting to return bodily for the final judgment and general resurrection of the human race. This life will fade into oblivion when every believer has the actual real experience of the beatific vision. The Latin term *visio beatifica* translated to English is "the vision of the blessed." It is the great hope of all believers, that in heaven we will see God as He is. Stephen had the experience of seeing the heavens opened, the glory of God, and the Son of Man. What a blessed vision of the resurrected Lord Jesus Christ and the blessed hope of our resurrection (Acts 7:55-56).

Life Everlasting

When Christians affirm that they believe in the life everlasting, they are repeating the Word of God. "For man goes to his eternal home while mourners go about in the street" (Ecclesiastes 12:5). The mourners represent people in this secular life. The word secular is often used by Christians and unfortunately it is often misused. The word secular simply means "this life" or "the here and the now." This life in the present time (the secular life) is from God. Simply because it is secular does not mean it is evil. Life has two dimensions, the secular and the sacred.

In the modern world, life is often thought of in terms of mere animal existence. When the Apostles' Creed refers to the word "life" it means that man is God's created creature. It also means that man was created in the image of God.

God gave special dignity to man by giving him the capacity and ability to think with intelligence and to make moral decisions. It is this rational capacity, moral ability, and emotional response that sets human beings apart from the rest of creation. When I comment that the greatest gift God gave mankind is rational ability, Christians often take exception. However, I quickly add that the greatest gift given to Christians is Jesus Christ. This special dignity given the human race to make rational intelligent decisions will never cease. It is not proper to say man is merely a temporary or secular being. Death does not bring an end to life.

The Bible teaches that the resurrection body will be like the resurrection body of the Lord Jesus Christ, therefore the resurrection body will no longer see decay, termination or death. The resurrection body will have an everlasting home with the triune God.

Given the fact that sin will overcome what is commonly called secular life, attention should be given to the concept of life from three biblical perspectives.

The first perspective is the secular life of the unbeliever. It is a life of darkness, an estranged life without fellowship with God. The secular life of the unbeliever is a life under the tyranny of Satan.

The next perspective is the secular life of the believer. It is a life of light with an intimate fellowship with God. The secular life of the believer is not free of sin, but sin does not rule over the believer.

The final perspective of life described in the Bible is eternal life or life everlasting and applies to all rational creatures.

Life is not mere existence, because the wicked will exist forever, but under the hand of God's divine justice. "And many of those who sleep in the dust of the earth shall awake, some to everlasting life, some to shame and everlasting contempt" (Daniel 12:2). There is an eternal life for the believer and everlasting life for the unbeliever. Eternal life for the believer is difficult to contemplate with our sinful minds. Jonathan Edwards explains eternal life for the believer with graphic language. "They shall eat and drink abundantly and swim in the ocean of love, and be eternally swallowed up on the infinitely bright, and infinitely mild and sweet beams of divine love" (*Works of Jonathan Edwards*, vol. 2, p. 29). On the contrary, to exist under the mighty wrath of God and endure the everlasting punishment is for the unbeliever. The Word of God describes it as everlasting contempt (Daniel 12:2). Those who belong to Jesus Christ not only have life, they have a blessed eternal life of joy and peace.

Daniel's prophecy is an awesome truth found throughout Scripture, but there is another passage of Scripture that should cause everyone to think about eternity. "Many are called but few are chosen" (Matthew 22:14). Such a profound inspired statement should cause every person to ask the question, "Am I of that number?" If we seriously ask that question and answer it honestly, it will help us understand the difference and desire for eternal life in heaven or everlasting life in hell.

Eternal life in a right perspective will help Christians put secular life in a proper perspective. Jesus makes a sharp distinction between the secular life and eternal life recorded in the gospel according to John. "He who loves his life will lost it, and he who hates his life in this world will keep it for eternal life" (John 12:25).

The first parents in God's creation lost their original happiness and blessedness because they broke God's covenant. It is the grace and mercy of God that restores that happiness and blessedness in the secular life of all those who belong to God through Christ. Then by grace Christians believe they have an eternal favorable relationship with God in the Lord Jesus Christ. He will bring the completion of salvation into ultimate reality when God's children enter into an eternal estate.

What will it be like for the redeemed, those saved by the blood of Jesus Christ, when at last they enter their eternal home? Ecclesiastes only states there is an eternal home, but in other places the Bible describes what the eternal home is like. "For behold, I create new heavens and a new earth; And the former things shall not be remembered or come to mind" (Isaiah 65:17). The former things that will no longer exist in the eternal estate are too many to mention, but for sure there will be no sin, no forgiveness, unbelief, pain, or misery. There will be no more time in eternity. With the curse of sin removed and with no more time, there will not be any more decay. I hate it when salespeople tell me a certain product will last forever. When you combine sin and time, every material substance will eventually decay. Even atheistic scientists understand this principle of physics known as entropy.

Many other former things will not occupy the attention the believer's eternal home. The source of light for the eternal home is the glory of God. There will be no more darkness. No more fear that you will be mugged or attacked while walking down a dark street, because there will be no dark streets. As the apostle Paul says, "eye has not seen, nor ear heard, neither have entered into the heart of man the things which God has prepared for them that love him" (1 Corinthians 2:9). The reason Paul says that is because our perception of reality is eclipsed in this sinful world. In the words of the apostle Paul "we see through a mirror dimly" (1 Corinthians 13:12).

The glorious nature and character of heaven is inexpressible because everything in this secular life is merely a shadow, type or figure of the full expression of God's redemptive plan. In the heavenly home Christians will know God perfectly thus they can love Him perfectly, not out of mere desire, but out of utter delight in His being. Think about what it will be like to be perfect and live in a perfect environment. Perfection means no sickness, no weariness, and no need to stop and rest or take a nap. Perfection means using the human mind to the fullest degree. It has been said that even a genius employs less than ten percent of his brain. In our eternal home our minds, not our brains, will function at a hundred percent level. People talk of 20/20 vision. The book of Revelation describes the splendor of the beautiful colors in our perfected state. The glorified child of God will experience perfection of all the senses.

Have you ever experienced loneliness? In our eternal home the sin that separates us in this secular life will be removed so that we will have perfect unending communion and fellowship with one another. Think of every mystery you've ever pondered and every passage of Scripture that never was fully understandable. In our eternal home all of it will be revealed to perfection.

When Christians think of an "eternal home" they immediately think of a house. What is your mental image of a house? The house plan you have in mind probably has an insecure foundation. Every house on this earth will eventually crumble because the foundation will give away. Your eternal home is different. The Bible says it is a city that has foundations. The King James Version of the Bible says our eternal home is a place of many mansions. We cannot conceive what it is like to live in a mansion that will never decay or ever need repair. We cannot conceive of the abundant space in our mansion. We cannot conceive the beauty and splendor of our mansion. The text in Isaiah where God promises to create the new heavens and a new earth should give Christians great joy as they anticipate their future eternal home. But for the present time Christians need to remember the rarely mentioned promise in Ecclesiastes: "For man goes to his eternal home, and the mourners go about the streets" (Ecclesiastes 12:5).

Every Christian should desire everlasting life. "The gift of God is eternal life through Jesus Christ, our

Lord" (Romans 6:23). The eternal home is not free. The Lord Jesus Christ paid a heavy price, so that the eternal home could be called "a gift" for those saved by the grace of God.

I hope you will agree that preparation for the eternal home is more important than anything else in this secular life. Christians will come to appreciate the thought of their eternal home as they contemplate the beauty of the everlasting life.

The Bible is the Word of God

The Bible makes it abundantly clear that all men know God, but what they know of God is not sufficient for salvation (Romans 1:18-21). The knowledge of God is natural to all people. The knowledge of God is both natural and general. It is natural because God planted that knowledge of Himself on every soul. It is general because of the indiscriminate distribution. It is a delight to find Christians starting with natural theology rather than denying it. Natural theology refers to the knowledge of God that can be derived from the natural world. However, the revelation of the knowledge of God in nature is not sufficient for salvation. Actually the revelation of God in nature only condemns the unconverted sinner.

Since natural man cannot find the gospel of the kingdom in nature, the Lord revealed Himself and His will unto His church. Those who are of God hear His Word for they are His people (John 8:37-47). God's people may take great comfort in knowing that God revealed Himself savingly, or as Jonathan Edwards says God revealed His Excellencies, to His people. God gave His people the Word of God so the truth about man's sinful estate and God's saving grace would be known to all generations.

The Word of God is a synonym for the Bible. The sixty-six books of the Bible are called the canon of Scripture. The canon of Scripture was not compiled under the inspiration of God, as was the writing of the Scripture. The books of the Bible were compiled by the church according to the grace of God and His generous providence. Athanasius of Alexandria (296-373) came to acknowledge the canonicity of the twenty-seven books in the New Testament. The Council of Hippo (393) and the Council of Carthage (397) affirmed the inclusion of the twenty-seven books of the New Testament and thus set the orthodox historical canonicity of the Bible. The church followed the fundamental principles for canonicity.

The authority of the book. Does it claim to be of God?

Is it prophetic? Was it written by a servant of God?

Is it authentic? Does it tell the truth about God?

Is it dynamic? Does it demonstrate the power of God?

Is it received? Is it accepted by the people of God? Does the questionable conform to the unquestionable?

The canon of Scripture is the recognition of the books of the Bible in plenary form. The canon refers to the reception of the books by the visible church.

Many professing Christians believe the Word of God is received by faith. The word *fideism* comes to mind when I hear people talk about receiving something by faith. The word *fideism* is rarely used in popular theological writings today, but fideism appears to be a popular view among evangelicals. The word *fideism* simply means "faithism." It means that the basis of reality is established by belief rather than what one knows to be true and supported by evidence. Persuasion to believe begins with evidence, not faith.

Therefore evidence and persuasion agree. For example, I am persuaded by the evidence to believe that Jesus Christ is the Son of God. The work of the Holy Spirit makes me able to believe the evidence savingly that my mind has persuaded me to believe.

The Bible provides abundant evidence which persuades me that the Bible is "the infallible truth." Then, does the persuasion come from my natural ability? Since my natural ability is sinful, the persuasion must come from a source that could not possibly sin. Therefore it is a work of the Holy Spirit bearing witness by and with the word in my heart. Jesus said as much to the unbelieving Pharisees, "Why do you not understand My speech? Because you are not able to listen to My word. You are of your father the devil and the desires of your father you want to do" (John 8:43-44). Without the Holy Spirit the evidence found in the Bible merely condemns the rational ungodly creature.

The Bible speaks clearly about God's glory, man's salvation and all that follows from man's relationship with God. However, the concept known as the "light of nature" is "that manifestation of God's will and man's duty which may be derived from external nature, from the events of providence, and from the mental, moral and religious nature of man" (*The Presbyterian Standards*, by Francis Beattie, p. 43). Often forgotten, but greatly to be remembered is that God's "invisible attributes are clearly seen being understood by the things that are made, even His eternal power and Godhead" (Romans 1:20). No human being can stand before God and say, "I never knew You existed."

Everything man needs to know about God is found in the Bible. Since God requires worship from all human beings it is absolutely necessary to know

God's nature and character in order to worship Him in spirit and truth. Christians have a sacred duty to worship and obey God according to the Word of God. God also requires human beings to formulate a world and life view based on the Word of God.

Some parts of the Bible are difficult to understand, but the salvation story is so clear and so simple that the learned and the unlearned alike may understand Holy Scripture. It does not take special training, academic scholarship, or the oversight of the church, because the rational mind of man is sufficient to understand the way of salvation taught in Scripture. Someone may come to understand the way of salvation simply by reading the Bible or it may be through the plain teaching of the Word of God. Of course, the knowledge of Scripture is not sufficient to save a soul. Only the Holy Spirit can enable one to believe the Scriptures.

Controversy is bound to occur among sinful people. Where must the church make its appeal in controversies of religion? First it is necessary to acknowledge that God inspired the Bible only as it was originally given to the writers of Scripture. Obviously Scripture was given in the Hebrew, Aramaic, and Greek languages, so the purity of translation depends on the ability to read and understand those original languages. Knowing the ancient languages will not insure an accurate translation, but a thorough knowledge of the languages is necessary for an accurate translation.

Many of the theological controversies that arise among Christians do so because Christians fail to study the original languages. Sometimes the way words are used in one language may not have a direct correlation in another language. Therefore there are occasions where an understanding of the original languages would assist in controversial issues.

The sure way to interpret the Bible may be found in two simple rules.

Context is king. This means to investigate the text from a grammatical and a historical perspective.

The more difficult passages of Scripture must be interpreted by the clear and obvious passages of Scripture.

These principles were the heart of the hermeneutic (method of interpretation) recovered by the Reformers of the 16th century. Context is necessary to bridge the gap from an ancient culture and language to our present culture and language. The second principle and equally important is that Christians must again recover the universal simple interpretative concept that Scripture interprets Scripture.

The issue before the church collectively is the authority for biblical interpretation. The Roman Catholic Church teaches that the church has final authority to interpret Scripture. The Reformers believed that the Bible itself was the final authority for all biblical interpretation. The watchword for this view is sola scriptura (Scripture alone). The Bible is infallible. The interpreter and the church are fallible.

The Bible translated into the known language of the people will give them the opportunity to see the message of God's absolute holiness and man's total depravity. Equally clear is the gospel of God's grace. The doctrine of God's saving grace is evident to Christians, who like the Bereans will search the Scripture for themselves (Acts 17:10-11).

There is a deeper question every Christian may ask. When doctrinal and theological disagreements are not settled, who is the final authority? The authority of Scripture by the work of the Holy Spirit speaking in Scripture is the answer. Therefore, new inspired revelation has ceased. The Holy Spirit gave the words to the authors of Scripture originally and those words still have the same authority and communicative power just as they were originally given.

It is not possible to have many interpretations of the Bible. It is absolutely necessary to have various applications from the interpretation of a text of Scripture. The one interpretation will have various applications. However, only one interpretation is the right interpretation, therefore controversies of religion will surface from time to time. When a religious controversy must be settled, the Bible must be the only and final authority. In spite of the claims by some modern Pentecostals et al, the corpus of systematic theology resonates with Scripture. The Holy Spirit speaks in Scripture, only Scripture, infallible and inerrant, not in the sinful heart of sinful man. The Holy Spirit speaks with judicial precision and legislative authority. The conscience of the individual Christian cannot be bound by anyone or any church court, but by Scripture alone. The decrees of councils and decisions of church courts are ministerial not legislative. However, it is dangerous to ignore the wisdom of godly elders who sit together to settle controversies of religion.

Reformed theologians are faithful to the systematic teaching of Scripture relative to interpretative theory.

Having done all in our power to compare Scripture with Scripture, to listen carefully to what it is saying, to criticize ruthlessly our own tendency to wrest Scripture, we can indeed approach the truth of the living God. . . .There can be no final court of appeal other than the Holy Spirit speaking in Holy Scripture. (*Westminster Confession of Faith Commentary*, by John Gerstner, Douglas Kelly, and Philip Rollinson. p. 24).

God's Eternal Plan and Creation

God is unique in every way and has a master plan for His creation. What has God planned from all eternity? The Bible teaches that God ordains whatsoever comes to pass (Ephesians 1:11). Immediately someone may suggest that God ordains evil. The word used to try to make sense of this notion is theodicy. Theodicy refers to the problem of evil and how evil came to be, but Holy Scripture vindicates God's justice. The Bible asserts that God is not the author of sin (James 1:13, 17; 1 John 1:5). It is not a contradiction to say that God ordained "whatsoever comes to pass" and at the same time say that God did not cause sin. This may be called a mystery, but not a contradiction.

God's ordination often leads Christians to think that the will of man is violated. God's ordination does not violate the will of man (Acts 2:23). Again there is no contradiction that God ordains all things, but at the same time God does not violate the will of the creature. This raises the question of human free will. The biblical principle is that man's liberty is not taken away just because God is sovereign, keeping in mind that God is the First Cause of all things.

The truth that God ordains all things is relative to the establishment of second causes (Acts 4:27-28), which may be contingent to our understanding, but God ordained such causes. It is easy to distinguish between the First Cause, God "ordaining all things that come to pass", and second causes, which work out in time and space according to human choices. The law of causality is the subject of gross abuse among some theologians, but understanding the law of causality is necessary for intelligent discourse.

It is a mistake to say that God's foreordination depends on His foreknowledge. The debate over the doctrine of God's foreordination and foreknowledge remains in tension among Christian theologians. The argument against the orthodox doctrine of God's foreordination is that God's foreknowledge is the basis for His foreordination. However, it would be out of character with the nature of God for Him to look ahead in time to get a glimpse of what will happen and then ordain it to happen on the basis of His alleged cryptic knowledge.

The Bible affirms the truth that God is independent, eternal, and unchangeable. Then it stands to reason that God cannot undo what he has ordained. To play these two words, foreordination and foreknowledge, against each other is a fundamental error. It is an error that may lead to all kinds of superstitious speculation. What God has established to take place cannot change, now or in eternity. It is a mute argument. Even common sense reveals that God must ordain all that comes to pass because it pleased Him and not merely because He knew it in advance.

The majority of evangelicals use the foreknowledge/foreordination argument relative to the salvation doctrine, because the majority of evangelicals are persuaded by Arminianism. The Arminian doctrine says that God ordained His elect based on His foreknowledge of those who would decide to accept Christ. This doctrine puts the final decision for salvation at the free will of man. To put it another way Arminian doctrine teaches that the will of man is more powerful than the will of God. Taken to its logical end it leads to self-salvation. It is the same old sin of Adam and Eve – self control. The problem with such conjecture is the fact that God is no longer sovereign, but is merely a puppet to the wishes of men. The Bible says, "as many as had been appointed (a perfect passive verb) to eternal life believed" (Acts 13:48). The language and the Greek grammar clearly make this an undeniable statement of predestination, not a suggestion that God based His decision on the decision of a sinful human heart. The clarity of Scripture shows that God created "every nation of men to dwell on the face of the earth, and has determined their pre-appointed times and boundaries of their dwellings" (Acts 17:26).

It cannot be denied that the Bible mentions words like election, foreordination and predestination, but the more difficult task is to understand the meaning of those words and what they mean in the mind of God. John Calvin alludes to not knowing "more than what is revealed in Scripture" relative to the doctrine of predestination (*Concerning Scandals*, by John Calvin, p. 53). Election and predestination are important doctrines, but it will require much more study, meditation, and maturity for Christians to discuss them intelligently and with charity. It is not my purpose in this book to explain the difficult and controversial details of these theological disciplines, but rather to give Christians a desire to study the doctrine based on the Word of God.

God accomplishes His plan in creation. The doctrine of creation has been another dividing doctrine among professing Christians for many centuries. It divides because it encompasses the unlimited power of God. Since human beings have a limited understanding of God, they are not able to grasp the magnitude of God's aseity. This word, aseity, refers to God's independent character. It is a word all Christians should learn because it sets apart the distinctive nature of God's being from all other created beings.

It is common for rational creatures to attach concepts to words such as power, wisdom, and goodness. People tend to think that God's power, wisdom and goodness is conceivable, because people themselves possess limited power and wisdom. Although the biblical concept of goodness is grossly misunderstood, man thinks of himself, in some sense, as good. Ask a person how they are doing today and many will say "good." However, goodness in the ultimate sense is the foundation upon which God's creative acts stand. The doctrine of Scripture teaches that in six days God created everything and all that He created was very good. Relative to this whole line of thinking is the goodness of God. Professing Christians would be wise to think in terms of man's badness and God's goodness. God alone is good (Mark 10:18). God created a good world but man, because of his rebellion against God, made it bad.

Did God create the world out of nothing? It is not common for rational creatures to think in terms of "nothingness." Although virtually impossible to describe, Jonathan Edwards made a stab at it by saying, "nothing is what sleeping rocks think of" (*The Rational Biblical Theology of Jonathan Edwards*, by John Gerstner, vol. 1, p. 123). The doctrine that God "created or made" the world (the material world) out of nothing (ex nihilo) is now contested by many liberal theologians. The "out of nothing" terminology means that God did not use any pre-existing material substance. He created out of His own power and from His independent character (aseity) a dependent creation.

The doctrine of creation is relative to the law of causality. God was the first independent cause, and everything that follows depends on that first independent cause. Causality explains the relationship between cause and its effect. Every effect must have a sufficient cause. It is a practical application of the law of non-contradiction. God is independent of creation thus it may be said that God is the first cause of all things which is often referred to as the first independent cause. The Bible teaches that God ordained everything that has or will ever happen. His ordination included the instruments and occasions which are called second causes. For example, God the first cause ordained that the apple would fall to the ground, but He also ordained gravity which is the second cause to bring about the apple falling to the ground.

God created man, male and female, consisting of bodies and everlasting souls. That one sentence is a summary of anthropology (study of man) from a biblical perspective. It may be true that many do not agree with this statement, but it is the teaching of the Bible (Genesis 1:27). Not taking the space and time to expand fully, let me mention two aspects of biblical anthropology.

First, God created man with a reasonable soul. Human beings have rational powers. They are able to think, formulate propositions, and satisfy the mind with a logical conclusion. Man's original estate was such that he would never have experienced confusion. Sin introduced confusion into the world, but sin did not destroy the rational powers of human beings. Christians should be careful not to deify reason, but they must not dismiss reason. They should exercise God's gift so they would be known as reasonable people.

The second aspect of anthropology is that the law of God was written in the heart thus man must decide whether to obey God's law or break God's law. This leaves every man inexcusable and establishes the basis for understanding the result of the sin of our father

Adam. The law of God written on the heart is what the Bible denotes as natural law. The apostle Paul says, "by nature [we] do the things of the law" (Romans 2:14).

The abandonment of natural law as a biblical concept by so many theologians has decimated the Christian worldview. The questions asked by the postmodernist may be answered by the doctrine of natural law.

God Provides for His Creation

Since God alone is able to create what He ordains, the Creator must be the Provider for His creation. The doctrine of providence means that God knows what His creation needs and He provides for His creation. God's sustaining hand is necessary for life to continue and have purpose. God is also the Governor of the universe. It is not possible for God to create *ex nihilo* (without any pre-existing material) and then leave the material world to its own course and purpose as the doctrine of deism teaches.

Deism during the 18th century tried to eliminate the evangelical doctrine known as the providence of God. Under the pretense of enlightenment rationalism the Deist acknowledged God the Creator, but not God the Provider, Sustainer, and Governor. Deism acknowledges the deity of God, but treats Him more or less as an impersonal force that gave laws to sustain and govern the universe. The modern whimsical idea is that chance is the means by which things come into existence. I may call it a whimsical idea, but renowned physicists and philosophers are advocates of such silliness. Chance cannot produce anything because chance is not a being and it has no power.

The doctrine of providence reveals the glory of God's wisdom, power, justice, goodness, and mercy. Providence reveals the material exhibition of God's character. The doctrine of providence in traditional evangelicalism affirms God's most excellent attributes.

Although God's creatures were created in His image, they lost the fullness of God's image at the fall. Therefore man is not only a dependent being; he is a sinful dependent being. God is perfect, holy, and independent in His being. Therefore, God can work second causes either ordinarily through providence or supernaturally without second causes.

Some creeds use the expression "ordinary providence" which simply means that God provides simple easy to understand events, circumstances, and visible contingencies to accomplish His greater purposes through second causes. For instance, God provides air, water, and soil to sustain an apple tree. At the proper time the apple will ripen and then God will use gravity to cause the apple to fall to the ground. These (water, soil, gravity) are called ordinary means or second causes in providence.

The Bible also teaches that God can work supernaturally or extraordinarily to accomplish His holy will. God can work without water to ripen an apple. God can cause the apple to ripen without any other material cause. God can even work against ordinary means, at His pleasure. For instance, God could cause the apple to fly up in the sky. It does not violate the character of God for Him to work supernaturally, but ordinarily He does not.

The Word of God reveals that God has worked miracles in times past. A real biblical miracle is a supernatural event that cannot be explained in natural terms. A biblical miracle is different than the common understanding of the word miracle. For instance, someone may say, "it was a miracle that I did not get hurt in an automobile accident." It was not really a miracle, but merely contingencies of providence working positively, according to second causes, to prevent what God had not ordained. The lack of Christian instruction and serious inquiry into the concept of causality has a sad watershed effect on the belief and practice of many evangelical Christians. It is always God's pleasure to bring about what He has ordained. Christians must remember that God's providence is the revelation of His generous care to His creation.

Acts of unrighteousness are typical of an unrighteous man, but what about the person who has been saved by the righteousness of Christ. Hezekiah was filled with pride, but the Bible says he "humbled the pride of his heart" (2 Chronicles 32:26, NASB). The providence of God shows forth the righteous and unrighteous acts of God's people for their own good.

God calls His people to trust His sovereignty even when the providence of God does not seem to favor them. When providence brings forth the testing of the fiery furnace, God's people should remember it is for their own good. It should remind them to seek God's will and pray for God's grace.

The way of the pilgrim is the way of the wilderness and until the pilgrim finds his home, God will chastise him for his sins and humble him to make him more dependent on God. Wicked and ungodly men still come under God's providence. It is called universal or general providence.

The Bible teaches that God does blind and harden unregenerate men while at the same time they harden their own hearts (Exodus 7:3 and 8:15). He not only withholds His special saving grace so they might have been enlightened in their understandings, and convicted in their hearts, but sometimes also withdraws the gifts which they had and gives them over to their own lusts, the temptations of the world, and the power of Satan. God furnishes instruments such as the preaching of the gospel for the salvation of some while the same means, preaching the gospel, brings damnation to others (2 Corinthians 2:12-17).

The providence of God does not ignore the unregenerate. The unregenerate reprobate cannot escape God's wrath. The apostle Paul said, "God gave them over to a depraved mind" (Romans 1:28). The Bible makes a distinction between the believer and the unbeliever. The Word of God is not ambiguous for it says "that which Israel is seeking for, it has not obtained, but those who were chosen obtained it, and the rest were hardened" (Romans 11:7). It follows then that they harden themselves even under the means which God uses to soften others. See 2 Corinthians 2:12-17 for the proof of this doctrine. This is difficult doctrine to understand, but Christians must not ignore the teaching of Scripture.

God hardens unbelievers because of their own lusts. It is because of the corruption in the sinful heart that causes the righteous Judge to give them over to a reprobate mind. The unregenerate, unbelieving, wicked person cannot and will not receive the saving grace of God. They are unable to believe and receive the gospel until the Holy Spirit changes the heart.

The providence of God has a particular interest in God's church. The Bible teaches that God's government and care extends to all people and all their actions. The Lord Jesus Christ explained that not even a sparrow falls to the ground apart from God's will. Even the hairs on your head are numbered (Matthew 10:29ff). It makes sense that if God orders something, then He must provide for the means to the end. The modern church has used the term "common grace" to define God's universal providence. However, God's people, Israel in the Old Testament and the church in the New Testament, have always been the recipients of God's special grace.

God's special grace begins with the operation of the Holy Spirit changing the heart thus enabling the renewing of the mind, enabling the will and sanctifying the emotions. The inspired Word of God says, "all things work together for good to those who love God, to those who are called according to His purpose" (Romans 8:28). God's purpose is providentially and actually good even when it seems that bad things happen to God's people. The special manner in which God provides forgiveness and provides for all things, including eternal life, is a real blessing to His children.

God's purpose in providence will bring His people to a close walk with Him according to His word. It is a special privilege indeed to come to the Lord with confidence and hope while we walk as pilgrims in this life knowing that God has prepared a special place to demonstrate His divine favor toward His people in the church now and the new heavens and the new earth later.

Basic Doctrine of Sin

Man was originally created free from sin, but still a dependent being. Man was originally created and placed in a perfect environment without sin, but man was mutable. He was able to make choices that would change his own mind, will, and emotions and his progeny. What happened? Why did man sin? Even in a perfect world man had responsibilities and sacred duties. God also gave man a positive law which was, "From any tree of the garden you may eat freely" with a stipulation that "from the tree of the knowledge of good and evil you shall not eat for in the day that you eat from it you shall surely die" (Genesis 2:16,17). Sometimes it is best to know the end, so the beginning will make sense. The introduction of moral evil into this world is one of those occasions. The Bible does not give an explicit statement on the origin of sin. Satan's temptation is part of the scheme and God's permission is certain. Theologians refer to God being active in the decree of sin, but passive in the participation. "Therefore listen to me, you men of understanding: Far be it from God to do wickedness, and from the Almighty to commit iniquity" (Job 34:10). God has chosen not to reveal all the particular details, however the temptation to sin comes from a sinful heart. The book of James explains that "each one is tempted when he is carried away and enticed by his own lust" (James 1:14).

To understand the doctrine of sin, it is necessary to examine the doctrine of the human will. These brief comments on the human will are worthy of your study and meditation. Every decision a person makes whether conscious or unconscious comes from that aspect of the soul called the "will." The will and the mind interface in the soul so as to constitute, with the emotions, the fullness of the human personality. The will has received so much discussion and debate over the past 2500 years that anything I say is not even a footnote. However, every Christian should endeavor to investigate this important doctrine for his or her sanctification. God created man with a will that was naturally endowed with the ability to decide for good or evil. Adam's will was not forced and it was not established to function by fatalistic determinism. Although many churchmen have investigated and written on the doctrine of the will, the two most prominent are Saint Augustine (5th century) and Jonathan Edwards (16th century). St. Augustine said that God created Adam and Eve *posse pecarre* (able to sin) and at the same time they were *posse non pecarre* (able not to sin). The first two rational creatures God created (Adam and Eve) had a will distinctively different than the rest of the human race since they were federally representing the human race. The result of the first sin changed the will so that man was unable to choose moral good that pleases God. If unconverted man should appear to choose moral good in his unconverted estate, he does so only to satisfy himself. Fallen sinful man's purpose is not to please God. Even though fallen man may appear to choose good rather than evil, he always chooses according to his natural ability in his fallen estate. The Pelagian doctrine teaches that man may achieve the highest degree of spiritual virtue by his natural will. Therefore, according to this doctrine, natural unregenerate people have the natural will to exercise faith in Christ. Arminian doctrine is close to this view. Although they believe that the guilt of Adam's sin was imputed (credited) to all men, they also believe that man was left with a spark of divinity thus having the free will to choose God rather than evil. They attribute the conversion of the sinner to God's grace while at the same time devolving the salvation to the free will of the unconverted heart of sinful man. The Bible speaks in terms of man's natural inability to contribute to salvation. The Lord said, "No one can come to Me, unless the Father who sent Me draws him..." (John 6:44). Again Jesus said, "without Me you can do nothing" (John 15:5). If the sinner could regenerate his soul or even contribute to that conversion he could boast in the face of God. A better understanding of the human will based on biblical doctrine means a better understanding of the doctrine of sin.

Total depravity is the term used by theologians to describe how original sin has corrupted and defiled every aspect of the human being. The mind, emotions, and will are corrupted as a result of the sin of Adam and Eve. The mind of man, being the center of his intellect, was darkened so that the moral and natural abilities of the intellect were diminished. The mind was not destroyed, but it was defiled. The will of man once faithful to God became rebellious and capricious. The affections once harmonious and delighted in the beauty of God became deranged and inflamed because of pride, lust, and covetousness. A summary of sin entering into the human race is found in Romans chapter five, verse twelve.

Sin entered into the world.
Death entered through sin.
Death was passed along to all men.
Therefore, all have sinned.

Paul the apostle describes the condition of the human race as being "dead in trespasses and sins" (Ephesians 2:1), "inexcusable" (Romans 2:1), and under the condemnation of death (1 Corinthians 15:21). The first human, Adam, acted as the federal head or the legal representative for the entire human race. The concept of federal theology is profoundly biblical. The inspired apostle Paul makes it very clear that "through one man's offense [Adam's sin] judgment came to all men, resulting in condemnation" (Romans 5:18). The theological term used to describe this is "imputation." It is a legal transfer of the guilt of Adam's sin to the offspring of Adam. It is not the transfer of the particular sin that Adam committed, but the guilt of the sin. The inheritance of the guilt of Adam's sin is sufficient to require the condemnation of the entire human race. Adam's corrupted nature is also conveyed to the human race. It is often referred to as moral pollution, which remains throughout this life. The grace of justification removes the guilt and the work of sanctification washes away the moral pollution by the most powerful work of the Holy Spirit.

The argument that people are born with original righteousness and favorable communion with God stands in direct contrast with the biblical teaching that all men after Adam come into the world dead in trespasses and sins. God spoke from His own mouth and said to Adam "Of every tree of the garden you may freely eat; but of the tree of the knowledge of good and evil you shall not eat, for in the day that you eat of it you shall surely die" (Genesis 2:17). This promise from God certainly intended physical death, but it also intended the spiritual death of a right and favorable relationship with God if man did not obey. The body and the soul were dissolved of the unity Adam once enjoyed. The sentence of death was and remains the unconquerable foe for natural man. The horrifying result of the sin of our first parents is not just death, but the total depravity that accompanies the death.

Basic Doctrine of Salvation

The doctrine of salvation is not a simple doctrine, but rather a complex doctrine. The doctrine of salvation is easy to understand, but it is connected with many other doctrines found in Scripture. The Bible says "believe on the Lord Jesus Christ and you will be saved" (Acts 16:32). The Bible also reveals a logical order of the causes and effects which produce salvation. Theologians often use the Latin terminology *ordo salutis* (order of salvation) to describe the biblical doctrine of salvation, which includes election, calling, regeneration, conversion (repentance and faith), justification, adoption, sanctification, and glorification. The order of salvation refers to the logical order of the causes and effects which explain the fullness of the doctrine of salvation.

Effectual calling is used to describe that part of the order of salvation that is first in the logical order. Our limited understanding of the application of God's grace must not keep us from our inquiry into and belief of this important doctrine. It is a calling that brings about the desired effect. Those who are effectually called actually come to faith.

Regeneration refers to the sovereign act of the Holy Spirit of God so that the children of God are given new life in Jesus Christ and enabled to understand and embrace the gospel. The Holy Spirit operates by divine initiative to give those who are dead in sin a new life in Christ which is called regeneration. Regeneration is necessary before faith. The regenerated mind and will are able to believe the call of God. The work of regeneration is strictly passive. The inspired apostle said it is the "power of God who has saved us and called us with a holy calling" (2 Timothy 1:8-9). Theologians freely admit the ordinary way of salvation is by grace through faith and usually by hearing the Word of God (Romans 10:17). God usually works by means or instruments; however He may work without the use of second causes. It is not out of God's character to act directly upon the souls of those who cannot hear the Word of God or understand the Word of God. It may be mysterious and miraculous to the human mind, but consistent with the character of God. The doctrine of regeneration changes the condition of the soul, but regeneration does not remove the guilt of Adam's sin. The guilt must be removed by an act of God which will be explained in greater detail.

Saving faith has historically been understood to consist of three constituent parts. *Notitia*, which is the grasping of the concepts inherent in saving faith, *assensus*, which is the affirmation that these concepts are true, and *fiducia* which means to trust based on what is known and affirmed as true. *Fiducia*, meaning to trust God for eternal salvation is critical because the devil himself understands the gospel, knows that it is true, and yet hates it. Likewise, the children of Satan may understand and know the truth of God's saving grace, but hating it they refuse to trust (John 8:42-47). Biblical faith is not a leap in the dark, or something to be contrasted with knowledge, but a conscious trust in the truth that can be demonstrated by the Word of God. God's saving grace is all a gift from God. Christians often say they "exercised their faith" for the saving of the soul. Every aspect of salvation is from God, even faith itself. The inspired apostle Paul says we are "saved through faith and that not of yourselves; it is the gift of God, not of works, lest anyone should boast" (Ephesians 2:8-9). Apart from the grammatical criticisms against "that" being a reference to faith, the logic of the language seems very clear. When the Holy Spirit of God renews or regenerates the heart, the Holy Spirit also produces faith. Man cannot produce his own saving faith. It must come from God. Believing that Christ and His righteousness are sufficient to save your soul is not enough. You must trust Christ to pardon you of your sin and accept you as righteous in the sight of God.

Repentance in the New Testament refers to the change of one's mind. The sinner has a change of mind then God calls the sinner to turn from his or her sin to God with the purpose of obeying God's commandments. The Greek word translated "repentance" as it is used in the Bible refers to a complete change of mind accompanied by a new design for living a godly life. The context is extremely important for understanding the meaning of a word. For instance, in Acts 11:18 the Bible speaks of a repentance that leads to life. In that context the word translated "repentance" encompasses the entire conversion experience. Repentance is intellectual and has an effect on the will so that a change of mind should be reflected by a change of behavior.

Justification is an act of God so that God declares the believer righteous. God judges the believer to be innocent based on the imputed righteousness of Christ. Justification is found in the Old Testament (See Genesis 15:6) and the New Testament (See Romans 5:1). The Protestant Church originally taught that faith was the alone instrument by which Christians were justified. Deviation from that doctrine occurred as the church denominated.

The Roman Catholic Church teaches that baptism and penance are the instruments of justification.

According to the Roman Catholic Church, baptism is a one time sacrament whereby justifying grace is infused into the soul. However, that grace can be lost by committing a mortal sin. The Sacrament of penance is the instrument by which justifying grace may be obtained again which is called the second plank of justification.

The salvation of the soul is the central aspect of the doctrine of justification. The word justification used in relation to the doctrine of salvation in Scripture is always used in a forensic (legal) sense. It is a divine act whereby God declares the elect of God, who are sinners and deserve condemnation, to be acceptable in His sight. The forensic (legal) language in the Bible explains our standing before God. For instance, "Who shall bring a charge against God's elect? It is God who justifies" (Romans 8:33). Paul's view is that justification stands in opposition to condemnation. Paul's judicial language describes and explains this important doctrine. The only way a sinner can be declared in a favorable relation with God is by the satisfaction of God's justice. Too often it is said the sinner's justification is free. It should be correctly stated that justification is a free gift. However the gift required payment and Christ freely gave Himself for that payment. The gift is free, or to put it another way, the grace is free to the recipient, but it was not free to the divine Son of God. It was Christ and His obedience and death that paid the debt thus satisfying God's justice. Although justification is more kairotic (point of time), than it is chronological (sequence of time), justification does have a lasting effect. In fact, if a sinner is justified, the result is eternal. Christians are not justified one day and unjustified the next day. Martin Luther believed that the doctrine of justification was the article by which the church stands or falls. He is right in the sense that there is no salvation if there is no justification.

Adoption is the grace of God for the heirs of everlasting salvation. The *Westminster Larger Catechism* describes adoption as "an act of the free grace of God." It should be understood that adoption is a legal act of God in the sense that it is something that God does apart from any merit on the part of the Christian.

The theological concept of adoption is explicitly present in the New Testament in the writings of the apostle Paul (Romans 8:15, 23; Galatians 4:5; Ephesians 1:5). Words like sonship, heir, and begotten are relative to the doctrine of adoption. The apostle Paul used the word adoption to describe the relationship a converted sinner has in the family of God. Justification describes a judge declaring a convicted felon not guilty. Adoption describes the loving relationship a father has toward his son.

The benefits of adoption include a particular marking by God. Those adopted in and for the sake of Christ will have the name of God written on them (Revelation 3:12). They will be marked as God's children. They are freed from the slavery of sin and taken under the care of a loving Father. Adoption as sons of God will issue an eternal inheritance in glory with Christ. All these and more are the privileges of the sons of God because they are predestined to adoption (Ephesians 1:5).

Sanctification is the process of being made righteous. I emphasize the on-going process in the doctrine of sanctification. The doctrine of the evangelical church holds that Christians are declared righteous by God the moment they trust in the atoning work of

Christ. The atoning work of Christ is the basis for believers to be justified by faith alone. Then believers begin growing in the likeness of Christ according to the biblical doctrine of sanctification. They become progressively more like what God judges them to be in justification. Sanctification is synergistic, a cooperative work between the individual and the Holy Spirit, who works both to will and to do His good pleasure. The process can proceed at different rates with different believers, but with all believers it does indeed proceed. The process is complete when the child of God is glorified. It does not mean Christians must be pure sometime before they die, but that at their death the process is brought to its end and then they are glorified. The biblical doctrine of sanctification teaches that a regenerate heart justified by faith alone breaks the dominion of sin, but there remains the presence of sin. This leads many professing Christians into a state of confusion. The result is often a life of uncertainty and residual dualism. The constant struggle to overcome the evil that remains in the whole man often leads one to believe that one may not be a saved sinner. The struggle is not a Gnostic form of dualism, but rather a struggle of the new nature against the old nature. The war will continue until death when the old man will finally be defeated. Christians struggle against sin. Unbelievers do not struggle against sin. Fighting against sin is a sign of new life in Jesus Christ. More will be said in Chapter 19 relative to the doctrine of sanctification.

Glorification is the final estate of the Christian's salvation experience. It will involve the full redemption of body and soul. The mortal body will take on immortality (1 Corinthians 15:53). Glorification will reveal the power of God over death, the final enemy of Christian believers (1 Corinthians 15:54).

Jesus Christ is the necessary axiom for any understanding of salvation, the forgiveness of sins, and the promise of eternal life. The apostle Paul, under inspiration of the Holy Spirit, asserts that Jesus Christ is the image of the invisible God (Colossians 1:15). It is the duty of every Christian to reflect on the nature of Jesus Christ. Reflect on the Prophet preeminent who reveals to His people by His Spirit and the Word the whole will of God. Reflect on the High Priest whose sacrifice is without blemish and is continually making intercession for Christians. Reflect on the King of the universe who rules over and protects His people. Reflect on the need for a Savior that promises eternal life.

Basic Doctrine of Sanctification

"Even if I knew that tomorrow the world would go to pieces, I would still plant my little apple tree and pay my debts" so says Martin Luther. I think Luther was keenly aware that he could not alter God's plan, but he could act responsibly to his call as a Christian. The Christian's responsibility before God is known as the process of sanctification.

The word sanctification (from the word sanctify) comes from the Hebrew word *qadash* which has the primary meaning "to be set apart." The Greek word *hagios*, which is translated in the New Testament as sanctify, has the primary meaning "to make holy." The meaning of the word sanctification is clear enough, but the meaning of the doctrine of sanctification is not a settled issue in the church. It is by the grace of God that Christians understand the doctrine of sanctification. This doctrine helps Christians better understand the concept of man created in the image of God. The doctrine of sanctification is about living unto righteousness.

The Christian was chosen to be holy. "For this is the will of God, your sanctification..." (1 Thessalonians 4:3). Paul goes on to say "God did not call us to uncleanness, but in holiness" (1 Thessalonians 4:7). God works according to His free grace to sanctify the Christian. Paul reminds all Christians that "He who calls you is faithful, who also will do it" (1 Thessalonians 5:24). God is sovereign in the work of sanctification. God must insure the sanctification of the saved sinner because man could never insure it. It is by God's sovereign free grace that sanctification takes place in the Christian experience. The image of God in man, defaced at the fall, is the reason that God must be sovereign in sanctification.

The inheritance of the defaced image was more than a demotion from the affluent upper class to the lower middle class; it affected man's relationship with God, and relationship with other people. The fall caused man to see himself differently than the way God saw him. God's system of justice requires absolute sinlessness. God declaring His elect righteous in the heavenly courts infinitely solved the solution. If God declared the Christian righteous, then why is man still a sinner?

Some of the 16th century Reformers replied, *simul iustus et peccator* (at once righteous and a sinner). God declares the converted sinner righteous, but the sinner is not made righteous. The careful observation of the words "declare" and "made" will help one make sense of this phrase. The process of sanctification is a life long endeavor.

Christians cannot claim ignorance when it comes to sanctification "because it is written, YOU SHALL BE HOLY, FOR I AM HOLY" (1 Peter 1:16). Sanctification should produce the fruit of the faith as Christians grow by the grace of God. Growing in personal holiness is like taking a walk and walking takes action. The compliment to God's sovereign grace calls all Christians to pursue a life of personal holiness. Personal holiness demands a cleaned up life. God has always expected cleansing as a part of His relationship with His people. God expects His people to consecrate themselves as a prelude to God's visitation (Exodus 19:10). The Bible requires Christians to make a conscious decision to pursue holiness "like the Holy One who called you, [to] be holy yourselves also in all your behavior" (1 Peter 1:15). Ethical expectations in sanctification must be measured in relation to the holiness of God. God's standard is perfection. "Therefore, you shall be perfect just as your Father in heaven is perfect" (Matthew 5:48). The standard is so high that Christians often confuse virtue, ethics, and holiness. The word "virtue" in biblical categories refers to moral goodness. Biblical ethics prescribe moral obligations. In his work on moral philosophy Alasdair MacIntyre argued that modernity should return to an Aristotelian ethic. MacIntyre, who claims to be a Christian, has confused holiness with a system of ethics. God's holiness is beyond the measure of an ethical system, although holiness encompasses the ethical realm. Christians ought to understand personal holiness in terms of the transforming character and conduct which takes place in the process of sanctification.

The 16th century Reformers gave careful attention to the doctrine of sanctification, but somewhere along the line heretical views came into focus. The primary heresy for this discussion is the heresy known as "perfectionism."

The early Reformers saw the depths of the depravity of man and realized that man could never be "entirely" or "completely" without sin and therefore never experience entire sanctification in this life. Kaspar von Ossig Schwenkfeld did not hold to the classical teachings of the 16th century Reformers, he himself being a reformer. He thought that Luther was misleading the simple minded uneducated people. Schwenckfel's early but influential teaching eventually led to what is known today as "Perfectionism." This heresy teaches that by the grace of God man will not make a conscious and deliberate departure from will of God or violate God's law.

The concept of Perfectionism has a number of adherents. The most significant are the followers of John Wesley in Methodism and subsequent groups who separated from the Methodist Church. The list includes the American Holiness Movement and the Wesleyan Church. Some Pentecostals and higher life advocates (Keswick Convention) espouse a form of Perfectionism. You will find various nuances of this doctrine within these movements. It may not be possible to untangle this maze of doctrinal disputes that divide the church, but it is the task of the Christian to seek the truth from the Word of God. The arguments for and against Perfectionism are primarily rooted in Romans chapters six and seven.

Romans chapter six is more than a contrast of the former life and the present life; it is a representation of the sanctification completed in the life to come. Paul is not speaking of a perfectionist idea in the Christian experience. Paul is just simply stating what is true for all Christians. Paul teaches that sanctification is the inseparable partner of justification.

Paul speaks of the Christian as a "slave to righteousness," but not in the sense of perfection (Romans 6:19). Romans chapter six teaches the principles of sanctification which are only appropriate for Christians. These principles are presented as the apostle gives us a contrast of the tensions that are particular to all Christians. For example, there may be times when sin seems overwhelming, but sin will not destroy the soul of a saved and justified sinner.

The two tragic errors that come out of Romans chapter six are legalism and antinomianism. The legalist is one who imposes rules or regulations that are not imposed by Scripture. The antinomians do not believe that they have to keep the law of God and therefore away with rules and regulations. The battle lines are generally drawn as Fundamentalists embrace legalism and Liberals embrace antinomianism with Evangelicalism as an observer. It has been said that Christians should seek to stay in the middle of biblical tension. The center of biblical tension is not legalism or antinomianism, but rather a positional and progressive view of sanctification. The classical view of sanctification teaches a contrast of these two concepts within a vital union to each other. The perfectionist was too quick to abandon the classical teaching. Romans chapter six refers to the completed work of sanctification, not in a present experiential sense. The facts presented in Romans chapter six come to life in Romans chapter seven. Romans chapter seven puts sanctification into the reality of the secular life and to that I now turn.

The position in sanctification is found in Romans chapter six, but the pattern of sanctification is found in Romans chapter seven. Romans chapter seven describes real life for the saved sinner. In the early part of the chapter Paul discusses the Old Testament law by illustration and explication. He defines sin and shows how it enables the Christian to know the clear distinctions between right and wrong. The apostle goes on to show that the law provokes sin and then explains the great battle that occurs with the Christian. Paul describes the inner struggle that takes place in the life of the Christian (Romans 7:14-25).

The text in Romans chapter seven has an age old controversy about it. The great argument is whether or not Paul is talking about a believer or a non-believer. Arminian doctrine would have a tendency to lean toward this passage speaking about a non-believer. Calvinistic doctrine would lean toward applying it to the believer. True interest ought to be in the doctrine of Scripture.

I am carnal (Romans 7:14).

That which *I am doing*, I do not understand (Romans 7:15).

I do what I will not to do (Romans 7:16).

I know that nothing good dwells in me (Romans 7:18).

The evil I will not to do, that *I practice* (Romans 7:19).

I do what I will not to do (Romans 7:20).

Wretched man that *I am* (Romans 7:24).

Grammatically, the verbs in this text are present tense verbs in the Greek. It means the action took place at the time Paul wrote this portion of the inspired Word of God. The great apostle Paul talks like he has a real problem with the sin in his life. It is an error to believe that great biblical characters are flawless. Paul not only studied God, he studied himself and when the character of God is compared to the character of man there will be a tremendous chasm between the two. Paul was aware the he was utterly hopeless without the power of the Holy Spirit working in him.

The apostle Paul has elsewhere discussed the concept of "babes in Christ" (1 Corinthians 3:1-2). A "babe" will not have much self control. Paul has already discussed the fact that Christians are still influenced by the evil one. The Christian struggles on the road of sanctification, but nonetheless makes a progressive movement on the road of sanctification. The Bible speaks about the mysteries of the faith and so we find a mystery in the process of sanctification, but the mystery comes to surface in Romans chapter seven. The mystery becomes experience. None other than Paul the apostle describes the experience. The language in Romans chapter seven reveals a deep sense of experiential indicators. The perfectionist says that Paul is not speaking of himself in this passage, but rather he is speaking of his former unregenerate state. This is rather illogical because it would follow that once Paul came to faith in Jesus Christ that he never struggled again with sin. The more Christians grow in sanctification the more wretched they sense themselves to be. The reason is the more they grow in sanctification the more they see the holiness of God.

The distinction in Romans chapter seven is that it is followed by Paul's affirmation that "The Spirit Himself bears witness with our spirit that we are children of God and if children, then heirs – heirs of God and joint heirs with Christ, if indeed we suffer with Him, that we may also be glorified together" (Romans 8:16-17). The Christian will suffer from the pain of sins throughout life, but in the final analysis Christians will be glorified with Christ Jesus. The process of sanctification is a victory. It is victory because Christians live in the Spirit. A struggle is not the indication of a defeat. The struggle between the flesh and the Spirit can be described as two opposing elements, one diminishing and the other increasing. Sanctification may be seen in that light as the progress of sanctification takes place in the present time.

Basic Doctrine of Church Government

The government of the church is under the supreme headship of Jesus Christ. It is well known that the headship of Christ requires a particular form of church government. The fundamental principles of church government are found in the Old and New Testament.

The principles of church government ought to be derived from the Word of God. Jonathan Edwards, although a Congregationalist, agreed with the Scottish Presbyterian minister, Ebenezer Erskine, relative to church government.

> As to my subscribing to the substance of the Westminster Confession, there would be no difficulty; and as to the Presbyterian government, I have long been perfectly out of conceit of our unsettled, independent, confused way of church government in this land; and the Presbyterian way has ever appeared to me most agreeable to the Word of God, and the reason and nature of things. (*The Works of Jonathan Edwards*, vol. 1, page cxxi).

It is true that many in the history of the church understand the guiding principles in Scripture, but practically avoid the practice.

The spiritual government of the church is not merely pragmatic or utilitarian. The government of the church is the source of order and authority for the church to carry out its purpose, mission, and ministry. It is for that reason that Christ has given His church a government to maintain order and harmony. It is well known that the church cannot do its work amid chaos and confusion. God is a God of order and for that reason church government must be prescribed by God, not by sinful man. Church government is no different that any other biblical doctrine. It is not sensible or rational to have two kinds of church government prescribed by Scripture. It may take long hard diligent study of the Word of God to understand and systematize the form of church government taught in Scripture, but it must be done. As with any other biblical doctrine, all Scripture must be considered, including both the Old and New Testaments. When Paul and Barnabas faced a dispute with the Jewish Christians they appealed their case to a higher court, to be more specific, a church court. They used the same principle found in the Old Testament when Moses appointed judges to "judge the people at all times" (Exodus 18:26).

There are four primary views of church government with a multitude of preferences among the four views. The earliest and probably the most popular is the hierarchical form of church government. This system also referred to as the Episcopalian system maintains a hierarchy of ordained men to govern the church. At the top of the hierarchy is the archbishop who has authority over subordinate bishops and they have authority over local leaders known as rectors or priests. The Roman Catholic Church and the Episcopal Church are examples of the hierarchical system.

The view held by a many Protestant churches in the United States is the congregational system. This system of church government places spiritual authority primarily in the hands of one man, the pastor elected by the congregation. Deacons are also elected by the congregation. In practice they may usurp the spiritual authority that is designed for the office of elder. This seems to militate against the teaching of Scripture because the Bible makes a distinction between the elder and deacon.

The third and less popular system is the representative form of church government also known as Presbyterianism. Dr. James Henley Thornwell, a professor and pastor during the nineteenth century explains that "the principle of representative government – of government by parliamentary courts, [is] composed of presbyters duly appointed and ordained" (*The Collected Writings of James Henley Thornwell*, vol. 4, p. 234). The Bible makes it plain that the churches in the New Testament had elders or sometimes referred to as presbyters. The apostle Paul appointed "elders in every church" so under inspiration from God there were a plurality of elders in every church (Acts 14:23). The Greek word *presbuteros* inspired by the Holy Spirit, most often translates into English as "elder." The word refers to those who had spiritual oversight in the church. Jesus Christ gave the elders authority to rule, guard, oversee, discipline, lead, teach, guide, shepherd, protect and set the example for the local church.

The fourth system and little known in the United States is Erastianism that teaches the state has authority over the church in all matters. This system is not biblical nor is it rational to give an outside organization authority over spiritual matters.

Biblical church government must have Jesus Christ as the head of the church. He rules His church through the instrumentality of men who are called elders in the church. The evidence from Scripture is that a plurality of elders is essential. It has been said "no elders, no church."

Therefore Christ appointed elders to rule over His church. These elders or presbyters rule by an ultimate standard which is the Word of God. In *Calvin's Catechism of the Church of Geneva* he asked the question: "is it of importance, then, that there should be a certain order of government established in churches?" The answer was: "It is: they cannot otherwise be well managed or duly constituted."

Churches are connectional and interdependent, not parochial or independent. Churches are ruled by biblical teaching, not by men. Elders fit the biblical pattern if they carry out their responsibilities ministerially, not legislatively. However extremes range from "tyranny" over the congregation to "no government" for the congregation. The old principle of truth and order are the beginning principles to establish the biblical form of church government.

Living by God's Law

The Lord God Almighty instructs His people to "keep His commandments." Those instructions are given by injunction from God on 52 different occasions; 42 in the Old Testament and 10 in the New Testament. The ability to keep God's commandments is conditioned by the ability to love God. Knowing the Law of God does not give one the ability to keep the law of God. Ability does not merely refer to an intellectual concept, but rather ability refers to an inward passion that drives a person to love the Lawgiver. Christians should study and meditate on the inseparable relationship between biblical love and the law of God.

Survey after survey reveals that professing Christians largely dismiss the need to obey the Ten Commandments. Pastors, teachers, and leaders are to blame for such behavior among professing Christians. Sermons dealing with the full nature, extent, and interpretation of the law of God have been absent from pulpits in this country for over a century. The gross abuse came with the introduction of anti-intellectualism, fundamentalism, and a liberal social agenda. This abuse accelerated as a result of under-educated and unconverted ministers preaching a wrong view of the law of God.

The law of God often referred to as "the law" may be explained within three categories. The first category is the moral law commonly called the Ten Commandments. The second category are the Levitical laws that regulated worship in anticipation of the priestly office of Jesus Christ. The Third category are the judicial case laws prescribed the punishment for violations of the moral law within the church underage, the state of Israel in the Old Testament. The moral law means the same thing to the New Testament Church as it did to the church underage in the Old Testament. Although the Levitical laws were given to Israelites in general and the priests in particular before Jesus Christ fulfilled the priestly office, they still have application to Christians today. For instance the book of Leviticus shows the holiness of God which is forever understood by His people. The judicial case laws are abrogated except for the general equity of their application.

The New Testament church has found three dimensions for God's law, commonly known as the civil, theological, and moral. The civil use of the law will restrain sin even among those who are not yet believers. The law is like a bridle that keeps them from turning down the path of utter destruction (Romans 2:14, 15). The theological use of the law of God convicts people of their inability to keep the law and thus drives them to Christ. "The law was our tutor to bring us to Christ, that we might be justified by faith" (Galatians 3:24).

The moral law, commonly known as the Ten Commandments, is specifically for believers. The moral law instructs Christians so that they will make progress toward a genuine knowledge of the divine will. The law instructs God's children and they will see and experience the benefits of His law.

God's people are special people and that is the reason they should keep God's commandments. Unbelievers seek grace in the law and never find it, but the believer not only finds grace but also joy in God's law. The difference is the believer finds grace where the unbeliever finds despair and desperation. God's people are set apart by the blood of Jesus Christ to keep His commandments and to love His divine law. This brief survey of the Ten Commandments is an essential part of Christian doctrine.

THE FIRST COMMANDMENT:
WORSHIP THE TRUE AND LIVING GOD
(Exodus 20:3)

It is proper to call the first three commandments the God-first commands, because they deal with the nature and character of God. The God first commandments instruct the people of God to worship Him in the proper manner. When the Pharisees asked Jesus, "which is the greatest commandment in the law?" Jesus responded, "You shall love the Lord your God with all your heart, with all your soul, and with all your mind" (Matthew 22:37). The essence of that command requires all the energy of body and soul to love the true and living God.

The first commandment is the foundation for all the other commandments, so it demands full attention by every Christian. The first commandment is the foundation for all religion. Human beings are worshiping creatures, therefore they are religious people. Human beings were created to worship God, but because of the fall they worship the creature rather than the Creator. The history of the human race is a history of worshiping people. The apostle Paul addressed the philosophers at Athens. It was a place and a people especially given to intellectual stimulation and with it the high culture of the day. Upon arriving in the arena, Paul "stood up in the meeting of the Areopagus" and brought up some of the observations of his tour of Athens. "Men of Athens! I see that in every way you are very religious. For as I walked around and looked carefully at your objects to worship, I even found an altar with this inscription: TO AN UNKNOWN GOD. Now what you worship as something unknown I am going to proclaim to you" (Acts. 17:22-23).

Today scarcely anyone would claim to worship an unknown god, but innumerable are those who worship particular, private, and public gods shaped by their own imaginations. All human beings including Christians are experts in inventing idols or false gods. All men do not worship the same false gods, but all men are guilty of idolatry. The Bible describes idolatry as forsaking the true and living God to espouse any aspect of creation. The concept of the term idolatry is self esteem, the spark of divinity, the center of creation, or it may be any other psychological, sociological or theological name. However, the primary false god within all humanity is self worship. God said to the ruler of Babylon, "you have said in your heart 'I am and there is no one else besides me'" (Isaiah 47:8). "I am and there is no one besides me" is at the core of human sinfulness. It is the primary false god of the human race.

The most important spiritual counsel for every Christian can be found in these few words: "You shall have no other gods before me." The true and living God must be the height of your adoration and trust. You must recognize His greatness as the creator, redeemer, sustainer, provider, and governor. God is the sovereign, almighty, eternal, triune God. For Christians to be faithful to this commandment they must know God in His attributes, His holiness, grace, mercy, faithfulness, and especially know Him in His Son, the Lord Jesus Christ. This commandment will give Christians the joy of knowing God in His Excellencies and enjoying Him forever.

THE SECOND COMMANDMENT:
HOW TO WORSHIP THE TRUE AND LIVING GOD
(Exodus 20:4-6)

God requires worship, service and obedience according to the pleasure of His good will. The Word of God is the way to know God's will relative to worship, service and obedience. God is a spiritual being and must be understood in terms of His spirituality. God is infinite eternal unchangeable and He possesses absolute holiness on one hand and absolute justice on the other. God requires that worship offered to Him must be in spirit and truth. For some strange reason Christian worship drifts off into idolatry. Idolatry is nothing less than the worship of human institutions. Idolatry turns the spiritual into the physical and the truth into a lie.

When God told His people in the Old Testament not to make an idol or any likeness of anything that is in heaven or earth, God was speaking to the church of all ages. The church must not seek to invent new ways to worship, for to do so will surely create human-centered worship which is forbidden. It is not your place to try to figure out what God wants. It is your duty to worship God the way He commands you and no other way. It is easy to make man the center of worship. For instance the preacher is either loved or hated. The singing is either good or bad. The organ is either too loud or the choir not loud enough. If "I" complains about worship, then "I" is the center of worship, rather than the true and living God. Is entertainment more important than understanding God's nature and character? If entertainment is more important then it is false worship.

The church collectively must worship God in spirit and truth, for His glory, decently and in order. The Bible provides abundant doctrine for the church to worship God in spirit and truth, for His glory, with reverence and adoration. The Bible is the regulative principle for worship. The full counsel of God reveals what is and what is not acceptable in worship. The following is a summary of what is acceptable to God.

Reading of Scripture.
Preaching of the Word.
Prayer.
Celebrate the Lord's death until He comes.
Confession of sin and faith.
Singing of Psalms and hymns.
Thanksgiving.
The benediction.

These elements of worship exalt God the Father, God the Son and God the Holy Spirit. Christians are commanded and ought to desire to exalt the triune God in worship, but often that is not the case. It was Jesus Christ, the second person of the Trinity, who said, "These people draw near to Me with their mouth and honor Me with their lips but their heart is far from Me And in vain they worship me Teaching as doctrines the commandments of men" (Matthew 15:8,9). On the appointed time on the Sabbath Christians gather and worship according to God's Word. That is outward worship. What really counts is the worship offered to God inwardly. It is called heart worship. It requires the right attitude toward the elements of worship that are conducted outwardly. What a great blessing to God's people when they worship the true and living God according to His commandments.

THE THIRD COMMANDMENT:
REVERE THE NAME OF GOD

(Exodus 20:7)

God's name reflects the sanctity of God's reputation. It is particularly important to understand the names of God. If Christians do not understand the names of God they will not understand His nature, character, or His will. Sometimes God's name is misused because of ignorance. Ignorance of God's supreme wisdom, infinite power, justice and truth is often the case when God's names are not understood. It is a common mistake to say "the name above all names is Jesus" and then quote Philippians chapter two verses nine and ten, but forget verse eleven. Verse eleven reveals the name above all names and it is Lord. Lord was the highest title known to the Old Testament saints.

The commandment is "You shall not take the name of the Lord in vain." The word vain comes from a Hebrew word that essentially means emptiness or worthlessness. God commanded Judah to stop bringing worthless (or vain) sacrifices to the worship service (Isaiah 1:13). This commandment literally means you shall not take the name of the Lord your God in a worthless manner. Worth implies value and there is eternal value in God's name.

This commandment teaches Christians to receive the Word of God with boldness and sincerity, because it comes from the name which is above all names. When Christians publicly profess the Lord to be their God, they become representatives of their heavenly Father. Therefore they must be careful to protect their Father's good name with their words and actions.

THE FOURTH COMMANDMENT:
THE LAW OF TIME MANAGEMENT
(Exodus 20:8-11)

The immediate reaction to this title may be "what an odd title to the commandment about the Sabbath." This is a commandment about time management because it is not merely a commandment about the seventh day. It is a commandment about seven days. The first principle in this commandment is about the first six days. "Six days you shall labor and do all your work." Maybe the reason this portion of the commandment is rarely mentioned by preachers and teachers is because many if not most professing Christians are grossly guilty of violating it. God commands believers to rest from their work, but also commands them to work six days. If "all your work" was done in six days there would be no reason or desire to work on the seventh, except to rebel against God's law.

The church has recognized the first day of the week as the Lord's Day for nearly two thousand years. Before that it was known as the Sabbath day. It is now called Sunday and once a year many Americans will call the Lord's Day super bowl Sunday. The Sabbath is the day set aside by the Lord of the Sabbath for His people to worship, meditate, and call upon the name of the Lord both in the public arena and the private closet.

Through the centuries the question has been raised as to whether or not God gave the Sabbath day as a ceremonial or a moral law. It was given as both. In creation the ceremonial aspects symbolize the redemptive work of Jesus Christ. It is also a positive moral injunction given by God for His people of all ages.

The word "Sabbath" is derived from a Hebrew word which may be translated "to cease from" or to "rest." It does not mean to become inanimate. It means to change or to cease doing one thing and go to another. When the Sabbath is used in relation to God's command to keep the Sabbath, it does not mean one is to be idle or lazy on that day. It means God's people are to perform holy works for the glory of God.

The concept of the Sabbath in the Bible is divided into three sub-divisions: The temporal, the spiritual and the eternal.

The temporal refers to those Old Testament sabbatical regulations given to remind the Old Testament people of God's holiness. The New Testament church also needs to be reminded of God's holiness. God established the proper worship at the right time. The New Testament church ought to follow the principle given to the Old Testament people of God.

The spiritual dimension of the biblical Sabbath is peace with God and cessation of worldly employments and recreations that are perfectly legitimate at the right time.

The eternal Sabbath is that in which God's children will be perfectly freed from their sins and the troubles of their labor in this life. The Bible says "there remains therefore a rest for the people of God" (Hebrews 4:9). True believers will enjoy their eternal Sabbath and have eternal rest in God.

THE FIFTH COMMANDMENT:
THE NATURE OF PARENTAL AUTHORITY
(Exodus 20:12)

The first four commandments are about God and the last six are about how God's people relate to each other. The fifth commandment is a transition between the first four and the last six. This precept says honor is due the father and mother from their children. God gave this commandment to maintain mutual order and respect for those of authority demonstrated within the familial framework.

When God requires fathers and mothers to be honored, God also demands that they discharge their duties in such a way to be esteemed worthy of honor. It means that children must obey their father and mother.

It is the regulative principle, the Word of God, that determines due obedience. It is from the Word of God that Christians should understand the law of authority. Christians must be certain, very certain, that they believe and act in accordance to God's law, because God's law is the final authority. They must obey that authority, because all true authority is based on God's holy nature and character.

If father or mother tells a child to disobey God's law, the child must disobey father or mother. If your employer tells you to lie or cheat in order to make a profit, you must disobey your employer. If the government tells you to abort your babies, you must disobey the government. If the church sets up its own rules, regulations, and authority that are contrary to the Word of God, Christians will have to decide whether or not to obey God or obey man.

Man-made rules and regulations that are contrary to the Word of God will bring havoc and suffering to the church and to society. Christians will understand the value of this commandment, if they understand the sovereignty of God. All ultimate authority belongs to God but He designates specific authority to maintain order in His creation.

THE SIXTH COMMANDMENT:
THE VALUE OF LIFE

(Exodus 20:13)

The word "murder" in the sixth commandment describes the act of taking someone's life (Mark 15:7). Sometimes it is used as a figure of speech (1 John 3:15). The word murder as it is used in the Hebrew text of the Old Testament does not always refer to the physical act. Every word in the Bible must be interpreted by the full counsel of God. We travel on dangerous ground when we ignore simple principles in biblical interpretation. Christians ought to consult the whole counsel to God to discover the biblical meaning of murder. It is a mistake to think that God is only concerned with the physical body and this present life. The Bible teaches that God provides for proximate matters in this secular life. However, the ultimate matters pertaining to eternal life are more important.

This commandment calls attention to the physical body and the important function of the body in this present world. Men and women are God's instruments that carry out His purposes and their bodies have to be preserved to be useful. The body is the temple of the Holy Spirit so we must treat the body with respect and prudence.

By consulting the full counsel of God, Christians will discover the application of this commandment that tells them not to murder the name of another person. Jesus gives a full explanation of this very dangerous crime (Matthew 5:21-26). It is cruel and vicious to murder a man in his name. The practice of gossip, slander, and back-biting by professing Christians is repulsive to God. The Bible warns the believer not to take delight in the misfortune of other people.

147

When Christians talk about another person's private affairs and especially a default or failure of some kind, they are guilty of the sin of gossip which is a violation of this commandment. Then there are those professing Christians who slander other people. A malicious false characterization of someone else is slander which is the murder of a person's name.

Anger, envy, and hatred are the primary sins that lead to murder. Unadvised and uncontrolled anger will seldom lead to the murder of the body, but will very often lead to the murder of someone's character. Envy is another sin that causes people to murder. It was envious Cain who murdered his brother. "Wrath is cruel and anger a torrent, but who is able to stand before jealousy?" (Proverbs 27:4). Hatred is another reason people murder other people. The story of Haman and Mordecai is a good illustration. Haman hated Mordecai because he would not bow to Haman. Do you remember the rest of the story? Haman sought to kill innocent people because Haman hated Mordecai (Esther 3:1-15). Hatred has ruined many a good name in the church.

Christians justifiably get upset when they hear about the mass murder of unborn children. Why is it that Christians do not get upset when people kill one another by thought, word, gesture and speech? As you can see, this commandment is not just an ethical code. It teaches Christians to respect a person and his or her name.

This commandment is particularly noticed in the public arena by unbelievers. It is tempting to tell an unbeliever about an immoral act committed by a professing Christian. Wicked actions like that destroy the solidarity, community and witness of the Christian church. This commandment is of the essence of Christian doctrine and the practice of it is essential.

THE SEVENTH COMMANDMENT:
VIRTUOUS RELATIONSHIPS

(Exodus 20:14)

The Old Testament has abundant references, mandates, and implied instruction on the subject of human sexuality. The New Testament is certainly not silent in respect to sex and sex roles, but the moral instruction is somewhat different. When sex is mentioned in the New Testament it is generally in relation to the spiritual life of the church. To the Corinthian Church the apostle Paul wrote, "It is actually reported that here is immorality among you, and immorality of such a kind as does not exist even among the Gentiles, that someone has his father's wife" (1 Corinthians 5:1). After rebuking the church for its immoral behavior Paul gives the reason for the rebuke. "For you have been bought with a price; therefore glorify God in your body" (1 Corinthians 6:20). Jesus Christ condemned adultery, fornication, and lust both inwardly and outwardly.

This commandment is a precept about the virtue of our own and our neighbor's bodies and how the two relate to each other. The moral duty in this commandment requires Christians to guard and protect their bodies against abuses as well as the bodies of their neighbors.

Adultery is evil, but it is no more evil than any of the other nine commandments. Unfortunately church leaders are more aggressive toward violators of this commandment than others. Punishment for this crime is often severe. Some Christians treat it as the unforgiveable sin. Some professing Christians treat this commandment as if it has been abrogated. It is the duty of Christians to keep this commandment, but it is a forgivable sin like any of the other commandments. It is the duty of all Christians who violate this commandment to repent and realize the greatness of the sin. Seek the boundless grace of God and ask for His pardon and forgiveness. And remember the words of our Lord to the adulteress, "Go, and sin no more" (John 8:11).

If sexual immorality is a problem, then somewhere along the way there has been a failure to work out the rules for right relationships. Forgiveness for the sin of adultery or for violating any of God's moral law is found in Jesus Christ and none other. David repented and found forgiveness. The immoral woman who wiped Jesus' feet with her tears and hair found forgiveness. Jesus said "her sins, which are many, have been forgiven, for she loved much" (Luke 7:38ff).

THE EIGHTH COMMANDMENT:
PROPERTY RIGHTS

(Exodus 20:15)

The commandment "you shall not steal" is habitually broken when Christians think that their possessions are more important than their relationship with God. The thief dishonors the name and character of God and shows no respect for God's generous providence.

What God requires of His children is that they honor Him first in all things. To do any less is stealing from God. In worship put God first. In your understanding the doctrine of Scripture and applying it to your life, put God first. In your stewardship, which encompasses all your possessions, including all the natural and spiritual gifts, put God first.

Many individuals and nations throughout history consider land to be the most precious commodity one may possess. No person on this planet owns any land. If you live in the United States the government, federal, state, or local will acquiesce and let you say you own some land, but if the taxes are not paid the land will quickly be taken away and sold to someone else who will pay the taxes. What individuals and nations forget is the Word of God. God gave the Israelites (the church underage) specific laws regulating the acquisition and disposal of land. "The land, moreover, shall not be sold permanently, for the land is Mine; for you are but aliens and sojourners with Me" (Leviticus 25:23). God owns everything. God simply grants certain people the privilege of stewardship of His possessions.

There are many ways that Christians steal from each other. The list is too numerous to enumerate every point, but I will mention a few. Stealing money or property from another person is a violation of God's law. It may be at gun point, by deceit or by default in a contract. Most of these are obvious, but consider this example. If I park in the parking lot and the person next to me opens the car door and puts a small dent in my car, that person has stolen from me unless he or she notifies me and pays me for the damage. First, it reduces the value of my car, which is theft. If I have it repaired then I must pay at least my insurance deductible, which ends up being theft. Hundreds of examples could be given to show that Christians regularly steal from God and their neighbor. People violate this commandment by slander and gossip or simply saying something that is not true about someone else. A person may be robbed of the truth, if preaching and teaching is not based on the Word of God.

Christians rob themselves by squandering the estate that God provides. They rob themselves of respect and dignity because of laziness, sloth, and wanting something without following God's plan for economic prosperity.

The Christian may ask why dishonest unbelievers prosper. Dishonest unbelievers may have more material goods in this life, but is that prosperity? There can be no prosperity without pleasure and all real pleasure comes from God. There is no real prosperity without being in a favorable relationship with God. Thieves must look to Jesus Christ, the spotless Lamb of God for redemption. It is the thief who understands the gravity of these words: "Today you shall be with me in Paradise" (Luke 23:43).

THE NINTH COMMANDMENT: THE LAW OF TRUTH

(Exodus 20:16)

The primary concern of this commandment is to understand and communicate truth. Christians cannot be part of the church without understanding truth nor can they be witnesses of God's grace without understanding truth. The Bible teaches that the church is the pillar and foundation of truth and that truth transcends time and cultures. "For His loving-kindness is great toward us, and the truth of the Lord is everlasting" (Psalm 117:2).

The commandment "You shall not bear false witness against your neighbor" may sound narrow in its scope and application. The word neighbor must be considered in the larger context. When the Pharisees asked Jesus, "who is my neighbor," Jesus responded with the parable of the good Samaritan (Luke 10:25-37). Your neighbor is the person who comes your way according to the providence of God.

What does it mean to bear false witness? This reflects the legal process used in Israel when a person must testify at a trial. The person on the witness stand was under oath to tell the truth about his or her neighbor. Speaking figuratively everyone is all on trial and God is the judge. His standard is truth.

Philosophically speaking truth may be measured within three dimensions.

Truth is the agreement with that which is represented. For instance a dog is a dog.

Truth corresponds with reality. It is well known that dogs exist.

Truth is conformity to rule. Dogs have certain characteristics.

Although philosophical inquiry is necessary, the most important way to measure truth is by God. Christians must measure truth by the nature of God. Although humans know God rationally by the innate knowledge of God and the empirical evidence in the creation, the primary and most dependable way to know God is through the words of Holy Scripture. The Psalmist says, "The sum of Thy word is truth" (Psalm 119.160). If the Bible is right, then the ultimate standard for truth is the mind of God which is written in the Word of God.

Private moral judgments do not count unless they line up with the Word of God. Moral truth is rooted in the integrity, trustworthiness, and faithfulness of God. Therefore, moral truth is an attribute of God. Holy Scripture commands Christians to keep God's moral law and truth is of the essence of God's moral law. Therefore, God demands moral truth from every rational creature.

Truth is essential for a culture to maintain moral integrity. When Israel was about to fall into the hands of the great King Nebuchadnezzar the Lord warned the people through the prophet Jeremiah.

Truth has perished and has been cut off from their mouth.

The prophets (false) hold fast to deceit.

The false pen of the scribe certainly works falsehood.

Everyone deals falsely.

(See Jeremiah 7 & 8).

Those words resonate with the contemporary church. It seems like truth has perished! This commandment demands truth to God, our neighbor, and ourselves.

The truth we owe God is absolute and begins with the primary responsibility to God which is to worship Him. The Lord Jesus Christ told the Samaritan woman at the well that "God is Spirit, and those who worship Him must worship in spirit and truth" (John 4:24). We owe it to God to worship Him truthfully. To worship God in any way not prescribed by Him in His Word is to worship Him falsely.

Our neighbor is entitled to the truth. Obedience to this commandment means you have to be truthful, honest and truth seeking in every relationship including, but not limited to, parents, children, spouses, co-workers, employers, employees, church members, and all unbelievers, whether friends or foes. The slightest deceit in dealing with other people or telling one lie or slander or gossip about someone is a violation of this commandment. To tell someone that the Bible teaches something that is not true is to break this commandment. To hold to doctrines that are contrary to Scripture is a violation of this commandment. Doctrinal indifference continues to weaken the once strong church in North America because Christians refuse to obey this commandment. Christians are starving for truth.

We not only owe God and our neighbor the truth, we owe ourselves the truth. Christians are confronted with truth, but they often choose to ignore it. How many times have Christians made vows or promised to do something and yet conscionably and deliberately fail to keep their promises. If they fail to keep promises, it is a sin against God, neighbor and self.

Liars have a father and his name is "the devil." When Jesus spoke to the Jews He said, "You are of your father the devil, and the desires of your father you want to do. He was a murderer from the beginning, and does not stand in the truth, because there is no truth in him" (John 8:44). Contrary to that father is God the father who gave His children the written truth, the Word of God, and the living truth, the Lord Jesus Christ. Satan's deception stands in stark contrast to the God's truth. From the Garden of Eden to the postmodern culture Satan stands behind all falsehood.

THE TENTH COMMANDMENT:
THE LAW OF GREEDY AMBITION

(Exodus 20:17)

There is a sense in which all sins can be traced to three root sins - pride, lust and covetousness. Of the three, covetousness is the queen of all sins. The first two rational creatures, Adam and Eve, found the sin of covetousness irresistible. "So when the woman saw that the tree was good for food, that it was pleasant to the eyes, and a tree desirable to make one wise, she took of its fruit and ate" (Genesis 3:6). The tree was desirable to our parents. The Hebrew word which is translated "desirable" in Genesis 3:6 is the same Hebrew word used in Exodus 20:17 as "covet." The Hebrew word translated covet or desire expresses the idea of a passionate pleasure. This commandment encompasses any inordinate desire to have something that God has chosen not to supply at a particular time.

The tenth commandment warns about the lack of contentment in the soul of man and the unseen condition of the heart. Covetousness is a condition of the mind, will and affections. Sometimes people refer to covetousness as greed. Its primary passion is an inordinate love for self and the apostle Paul said men will be lovers of self (2 Timothy 3:2). This is the sin that wants the reputation of another man, but the coveter is unable to gain the other persons good charac-ter so he slanders the other person in an attempt to raise his own ego. Coveting is evident when people do not have certain material things, so they steal because the heart covets the things of this world. Sometimes people will not discipline themselves to think intelligently, so they tell lies to try and impress people, because they covet attention. Covetousness is an inward problem that requires an inward change by the power of the Holy Spirit to improve this condition.

The covetous man takes great pain to gain the things of this world and cares little, if any, about eternal life and the heavenly home. The covetous man spends his time talking about this world. The covetous man is more interested in the business world, the sports world, the recreation world, and in short his own world rather than God's world now and eternally.

Only one man did not commit the sin of covetousness, the Lord Jesus Christ. "For He [God] made Him [Jesus Christ] who knew no sin to be sin for us, that we might become the righteousness of God in Him" (2 Corinthians 5:21).

The great Christian hope is to believe that Jesus is the Son of God through faith alone. Jesus Christ the sinless is the Savior. All men are called to receive Him by grace alone for the salvation of the soul.

THE APPLICATION OF GOD'S LAW IN CHRISTIAN RELATIONSHIPS

The one another commandments in Scripture describe how Christians have a duty to apply the Ten Commandments in everyday life. They summarize the way Christians ought to live. These one another commandments in the New Testament amplify the second table of the Ten Commandments. A summary of the one another commandments will help Christians understand the significance of living the doctrine they believe. The following summarize the one another commandments.

Love one another (John 13:34).
Receive one another (Romans 15:7).

Encourage one another (1Thessalonians 5:11).
Bear one another's burdens (Galatians 6:2).
Teach one another (Colossians 3:16).
Submit to one another (Ephesians 5:21).
Admonish one another (Romans 15:14).
Peace with one another (Mark 9:50).
Be kind to one another (Romans 12:10).
Wait for one another (1 Corinthians 11:33).
Serve one another (Galatians 5:13).
Bear with one another (Ephesians 4:2).
Be hospitable to one another (1 Peter 4:9).
Give preference to one another (Romans 12:10).
Greet one another (Romans 16:16).
Do not speak evil of one another (James 4:11).
Do not lie to one another (Colossians 3:9).

Although this list is not complete it is sufficient to remind Christians of their responsibility toward each other based on their relationship with the triune God. Please notice that these are reciprocal commands. From the Greek text we learn that the English words "one another" come from one Greek word which is a plural pronoun. It simply means that "one another" includes everyone that belongs to Jesus Christ.

The Holy Spirit not only enables Christians to have a relationship with God through the work of Christ, He enables Christians to have a relationship with one another. If Christ accepted us when we were weak and deserved death, then how should we accept one another? It may be necessary to put aside petty differences of opinion especially if the opinion is not grounded in the Word of God. However, the principles and precepts in the Word of God are not negotiable.

The one another commandments are given because converted sinners are still sinners. Right relationships with other Christians are not obstructed by sound biblical doctrine, but rather by the sin nature that elevates self above others. When "I" is the center of all being and expression, then the relationship changes from "one another" to "I am." The Bible explains the condition of the human race in terms of "I am and there is no one besides me" (Isaiah 47:8). The "I am" in that text refers to the king of Babylon who believed that he was above all men and even above God. The zenith of sin is self centeredness. I am, I want, I will, I did, I was, I, I, I is the basic pattern of man-centeredness. The evil one delights in people being in bondage to the self centeredness. This sin leads to individualism and the desire to be independent of God. It naturally follows that God commands His child to purge "I am" and replace it with "one another". Obedience to all the commandments in Scripture requires love for God and love for the saints of God.

HOW TO LIVE LOVING ONE ANOTHER

A little girl said to her Mother, "Mommy I love my baby dolls, but they don't love me back." The word love is probably one of the most misunderstood and misused words in the modern world. During my undergraduate studies I was involved in a research project, part of which was to ask teenagers this question: What is love? Many of them referred to love as a "feeling." A majority of them (87%) were Christians but they never referred to any aspect of love from a biblical perspective.

The word love is used often in the Bible, but more often in the New Testament. Love is difficult to define. When used as a noun it is an abstract word because it transcends the senses. When love is used as a verb it often has in mind the idea of a relationship to someone and something.

The first time the word love is used in the Old Testament it describes Abraham's affectionate relationship with his only son Isaac (Genesis 22:2). The last use of the word love in the Old Testament is a mandate from the Lord to "love truth and peace" (Zechariah 8:19). Likewise in the New Testament love is associated with relationships, affections and truth. The meaning of love is not limited to human emotions, but rather love comes from the mind and the will of the soul. The extent of its meaning is sometimes best understood when compared to the opposite end of the spectrum; love stands in opposition to hate. Love and hate are basic attitudes of life. "Hatred stirs up dissension, but love covers over all wrongs" (Proverbs 10:12).

The apostle Paul describes love as the most excellent way (1 Corinthians 13). The most excellent way hopes all things, endures all things and never fails. Did Paul say "love never fails?" Paul describes love biblically, while the contemporary culture defines love in terms of affection, approval, attraction, and so on but they all fail at some point. When Paul says that love never fails he must mean divine love. The love of God never fails. The love people have for one another fails to a greater or lesser degree at one time or another.

Jesus issued the commandment to love one another, which is related to the Old Testament commandment to "love your neighbor as yourself" (Leviticus 19:18). Jesus issued this commandment because love was a principle that He lived and died for. The love of Christ is pure love and it is free of prejudice. He prayed for the ones who murdered him because His love for them was free of prejudice.

Jesus gave the commandment to love one another because it would show evidence of the new spiritual birth. "We know that we have passed from death to life because we love our brothers" (1 John 3:14). Spiritual regeneration is one of the theological implications of brotherly love. It is also evidence of spiritual growth.

Love one another is a reciprocal command. Christians must mutually love each other. The injunction to love one another ought to be the desire of the heart; Not under compulsion, but freely with a merciful heart. The following are a few of the verses that will remind Christians of their responsibility to love one another.

New command (John 13:34).
Mark of Christianity (John 13:35).
Love each other as Jesus loves (John 15:12).
Christ commands Love   for each other (John 15:17).
Fulfill the law – love each other (Romans 13:8).
Let love overflow for each other (1 Thessalonians 3:12).
Taught by God to love each other (1 Thessalonians 4:9).
Love one another deeply from the heart (1 Peter 1:22).
Message from the beginning love one another (1 John 3:11).
Faith and love are commandments (1 John 3:23).
Evidence of Christianity (1 John 4:7).
Since God loved we ought to love one another (1 John 4:11).
Evidence of Christianity (1 John 4:12).
Challenge to love one another (2 John 1:5).

If Christians meditate on the command to "love one another" it will always lead to the desire for the well being of the other person. Rather than acting on self interest Christians that love one another will act in the sole interest of the other person.

Love is inseparably connected with other aspects of the Christian life. It has been said that love is the father of justice. Justice requires pure and true love which is found in the Lord Jesus Christ. If love is the father of justice, then love is the mother of truthfulness. Christians are not able to deceive those they truly love. The connection between truth and love is inseparable. Love comes before mercy and gives the faint hearted patience to finish the race. Love is the main spring that gives the believer courage and strength to follow God.

Christians must love God in response to His love for them, and they are to love each other as a result of their love for God. "We love, because He first loved us. If someone says, 'I love God,' and hates his brother, he is a liar; for the one who does not love his brother whom he has seen, cannot love God whom he has not seen. And this commandment we have from Him, that the one who loves God should love his brother also" (1 John 4:19–21, NASB).

Love is the energy of the soul expressed by human affections and action directed to the beloved. Jonathan Edwards made a statement about love that comforts the soul. "But when love is in lively exercise, persons don't need fear, and the prevailing of love in the heart, naturally tends to cast out fear" (*Letters and Personal Writings of Jonathan Edwards*, Yale edition vol. 16, p. 94,).

HOW TO LIVE ENCOURAGING ONE ANOTHER

Why would Christians have to be commanded to encourage one another? It seems like they would want to be encouraged. The answer is yes, they want to be encouraged and that is the core of the problem. The modern church has become dependent on the "meet my needs" agenda, rather than encouraging one another. In Paul's letter to the Thessalonians The New American Standard Bible reads "encourage one another" and the New King James Version reads "comfort one another" (1 Thessalonians 5:11). The Greek word *parakaleo* literally means "to call by the side or to call near" and is translated "encourage" or "comfort." The implication is that one Christian is called to stand beside the other and visa versa. Encouragement and comfort will always result when someone stands beside you.

Christians need to encourage one another for many reasons. Encouragement is needed because the Word of God says, "all who desire to live godly in Christ Jesus will suffer persecution" (2 Timothy 3:12). The promise from Scripture is that a godly compassionate relationship with other Christians will bring comfort and relief. When Christians experience various and sundry troubles in life (Job 5:7), the need to encourage one another is the balm of relief.

One of the great needs in the church today is encouraging one another with sound doctrine. The apostle Paul charged Timothy to "Hold fast the pattern of sound words which you have heard from me, in faith and love which are in Christ Jesus" (2 Timothy 1:13). This verse has three grammatical considerations when examined separately will help Christians understand the entire verse.

The command is have or to hold fast.

The pattern is a summary account or an outline.

Sound words are healthy words, good for the health of the soul.

Paul literally says have an outline of healthy words which you have heard from me. The only way Christians should teach one another is with sound doctrine and that requires using sound words. The sound words found in the Word of God are good for the soul. Therefore, healthy words from the Word of God will result in a healthy soul when Christians receive them in faith and love. The Word of God is the best way to encourage one another.

HOW TO LIVE PRAYING FOR ONE ANOTHER

The Book of James commands Christians to "pray for one another" (James 5:16). Although this is in the form of a commandment, the evidence from the corpus of Scripture is that Christians should pray for one another without being commanded by God. The essential meaning of the word pray and prayer is to call on God or go before God in confession, praise and petition. Prayer for one another should reflect the interest each one has for the sanctification of the other. Unfortunately some professing Christians return to God with prayer only in the case of an emergency when all other efforts to protect life or property fail. There are times when it is a sin to pray for one another. "And whenever you stand praying, if you have anything against anyone, forgive him, that your Father in heaven may also forgive you your trespasses. But if you do not forgive, neither will your Father in heaven forgive your trespasses" (Mark 11:25). The inspired Psalmist said, "If I regard iniquity in my heart, the Lord will not hear [my prayer]" (Psalm 66:18). An unforgiving heart that loves sin will not be heard by God simply because there is no Mediator between sinful man and holy God. Confess, forgive, repent and restore is the pattern found in Scripture so that God will hear the prayers offered in the name of Christ for one another.

The "pray for one another" doctrine is found in the Lord's model prayer. Jesus said the model for prayer is "our Father...give us...our daily bread...lead us...deliver us" (Luke 11:1-4). It is not me or mine, but rather a mutual concern that causes "us" to pray for one another. The commandment is "pray for one another," Christians ought to delight in praying for the members in the family of God.

HOW TO LIVE IN RIGHT RELATIONSHIPS TO ONE ANOTHER

The apostle Paul addresses the doctrine of living in a right relationship with one another in the book of Ephesians (5:15 – 6:9). The text explains how husbands and wives, children and parents, and servants and masters should "submit to one another in the fear of the Lord" (Ephesians 5:21). The idea of submitting to one another is relative to mutual obedience. God places every person in a particular order to maintain right relationships. The top of all relationships begins with Jesus Christ. Christians submit to one another because of their relationship to and reverence for the Lord Jesus Christ.

165

The whole counsel of God explains how to have a right relationship with others, thus submitting to one another. It is not possible to submit to one another and not follow the management and role order that God has assigned to the family unit. It is not possible to submit to one another and not submit to the economic station in life that God ordained for one another.

The enemies to right relationships with each other in the body of Christ are many, but a few deserve special attention. Self-centeredness will never submit to one another. A person that is self-centered is governed by the thought that everything revolves around him or her. Unless God is at the center of the relationship it will not be a right relationship. Another enemy to mutual submission is the person with a dictatorial attitude. Since their purpose is to lord it over others, they are unable to submit even in the fear of the Lord. Thoughtlessness is another enemy of mutual submission because a thoughtless person has no respect for the position, needs, desires and welfare of others. All of these enemies to mutual submission will prevent right relationships.

The only way to submit to one another is to agree on the doctrine of Scripture. For instance, if the husband has a false view of Jesus Christ, then the husband should not expect his wife to submit to him. If the employer has a false view of Christ he should not be disturbed if the employee does not submit to ungodly demands. The principle is that false doctrine will always militate against mutual submission and right relationships. It is wise to be generous when a brother or sister disagrees on some aspect of biblical doctrine, but it is unwise to accommodate yourself to wrong teaching and false doctrine. It is then that prayer,

encouragement, and love will prevail in the relationship.

HOW TO LIVE BEARING ONE ANOTHER'S BURDEN

Over the past thirty years I've heard numerous
sermons or Sunday School lessons on the text from
Galatians that says "bear one another's burdens" plus a
multitude of casual references to this one another
commandment. This commandment has suffered
interpretative abuse because it was taken out of context.
The context (Galatians 5:26 - 6:10) calls one another to
help restore those who are burdened by sin. That would
include all Christians, thus one another in the plural.

Christians burdened by sin have no trouble finding other Christians that are more than willing to
criticize and find fault. Then others are calling for
punishment rather than restoration of a fallen brother or
sister. Of course there are plenty who simply ignore a
fallen brother or sister. The biblical way to bear one
another's sin burden is to be restored by those who are
spiritual (Galatians 6:1, 2). Christians fulfill the law of
Christ by bearing one another's sin burden. The law of
Christ says "love one another; as I have loved you"
(John 13:34). Christ certainly took away the sin burden
of the people who belong to Him.

How do we apply this commandment "bear one
another's burden?" First the Christian must evaluate
his or her own life. Do Christians reflect love and joy
in our relationship with other Christians and even
unbelievers. The self examination must also include
peace, kindness, goodness, faithfulness, gentleness and
self-control. The fundamental idea is that Christians
must bear one another's burdens with humility, gentle-

ness, and compassion. I remember hearing an illustration about a surgeon telling a patient "I may hurt you, but I will not injure you." Obeying this command may not be easy, but if it is carried out God's way it will bring great joy to the body of Christ.

The Nature of a Christian

It is not enough to know and believe the essential doctrine of the Christian religion. Christians are called to live according to their faith. A new creature in Christ will have a new outlook on life because it is a new life. The essential characteristics of Christians, truly professing and practicing Christians, are outlined in the beatitudes (Matthew 5:3-11). The Sermon on the Mount, as it is commonly called, is for God's children. The beatitudes define a Christian.

The ethical dimension of the Sermon on the Mount is the primary interest for many Christians. Teachers may overlook the indicative dimension of the Beatitudes. The indicative dimension refers to the essence of Christianity rather than the practice of Christianity. The ethical dimension is about doing while the indicative refers to being.

Christianity is bi-dimensional. First, Christianity is a state of being, which I refer to as the indicative dimension. The second dimension of Christianity is a state of doing, which I refer to as the ethical dimension. Christians are "doing" what God calls them to do because God has given a new state of being in Jesus Christ. The beatitudes describe this state of being. When Jesus said "Blessed are the poor in spirit" it describes a condition of the believer, not something the believer is commanded to do. These blessings, also called beatitudes, give the believer an understanding of the nature of a Christian. When Jesus said blessed are the poor in spirit, He is describing the nature of a Christian.

When Jesus announced the "blessings" in Matthew chapter five, He ended them by saying

"Blessed are those who have been persecuted for the sake of righteousness... ." Persecution comes because natural man hates God. "The wrath of God is being revealed from heaven against all the godlessness and wickedness of men who suppress the truth by their wickedness" (Romans 1:18). Jonathan Edwards said "man is naturally totally ignorant of God in His divine Excellency." Edwards is not saying that natural man is totally ignorant of God, but totally ignorant of the majesty of the divine Excellency of God. Every human has some knowledge of God. Those who have not been born again by the Spirit of God hate what they know about God. Those who have been spiritually re-born by the Spirit of God have a saving knowledge of God's sweetness and Excellency. The Christian is then blessed according to the nine benedictions given by Jesus in the Beatitudes.

A person who has been blessed should become a blessing to others. If you are a Christian, you're like salt and light. If a believer is truly blessed by the life changing power of the Holy Spirit, then the believer will desire to be a blessing by doing what Christ commands. Jesus describes what Christians are like in response to a society that hates God and seeks to persecute God's servants. Jesus used two metaphors, salt and light, to describe a Christian. If you are like salt and light, then your actions will reflect your state of being. A horse acts like a horse, because a horse is a horse. It is a simple statement, but it is loaded with philosophical and theological profundity. It sounds so simple, let's try another statement. A Christian acts like a Christian because a Christian is a Christian. Jesus explains why in the Gospel of Matthew (Matthew 5:13-16).

Jesus said, "you are the salt of the earth" (Matthew 5:13). Obviously this is not a literal statement, because a Christian is more than a chemical composition known as sodium chloride. The word salt found in Scripture has many qualities. It may be used to flavor and season food, to preserve and cleanse, and to render useless. It is also used as a figure of speech. Jesus referred to "salt" as a figure in this text to describe those Christians who act as a preservative in society. Salt not only preserves, it nourishes. Christians serve as a means of spiritual nourishment to a deprived and depraved society. Salt also symbolically serves as an agent to make land unproductive. Christians will make the works of Satan unproductive by teaching and preaching the truth from God's Word while they pray for reformation. Finally, salt creates thirst. Are you a salty Christian? Do you stand for truth? Most Christians say they believe the truth, but can they defend the truth? I don't know what the statistics are now, but about 15 years ago there were reportedly 60 million evangelical Christians in the United States. If that is true, where is the evidence? Where is the salt?

Jesus said, "you are the light of the world" (Matthew 5:14). He goes on to say you are the light if you "let your light shine before men, that they may see your good works..." (Matthew 5:16). Natural man is in spiritual darkness, but the person who is born again by the Spirit of God is walking in the light and it must show. Jesus puts it in the form of a command, "Let your light shine before men." When Christians hide their righteousness from the unconverted person the light is no longer shining. When Christians hide their righteousness from the converted person who might mock their Christian walk, the light is out. Children of God should say like the Psalmist, "My heart shall rejoice in Thy salvation" (Psalm 13:5). One way to experience the joy of salvation is to be salt and light in an unsavory and dark world.

Christians are blessed because they do not have to struggle for identity. Their identity is in their source of being, the Lord Jesus Christ. By the grace of God, the love of Christ, and the power of the Holy Spirit, Christians will rejoice that they know who they are and how to live.

Biblical Evangelism

Christian evangelism is part of the Christian worldview. Christians must take some part in announcing the good news of salvation. Many questions have been asked about evangelism. What is the message of evangelism? What is the right method of evangelism? What is the goal of evangelism? Where is the mandate for evangelism? Although every question is important, Christians must first be certain that the concept of evangelism is a discipline in Christian theology. Evangelism is not the purpose of the church. The purpose of the church is to worship God. Evangelism is part of the mission and ministry of the church. There is a curious notion among many evangelicals that the primary duty of the church is evangelism.

Many of the 16th through the 18th century evangelists apparently considered the task of evangelism at face value. In other words, it was part of their world and life view. There is no indication from the Book of Acts that the early Christians had to pin someone to the wall and present the gospel by using steps a, b, c, and a prayer of declaration. Evangelism was part of their daily life.

There are plenty of books on evangelism that I would not recommend to lay theologians, but, I would recommend *God-Centered Evangelism* by R. B. Kuiper or *Evangelism and the Sovereignty of God* by J. I. Packer. However, the Bible should be the primary source to understand the doctrine of evangelism.

Evangelism is probably the most misunderstood and abused doctrine in the modern church. My experience with evangelistic messages and methods used in the modern church is that the sinner is required to do something to contribute to the salvation of the soul. Maybe it was a prayer or going to the front of the church during an altar call or coming forward in a crusade? After a serious and searching inquiry into the Word of God, it became abundantly clear to me that an unconverted soul could not do anything to save himself or herself.

The Bible has abundant evidence revealing that all people are born with a sinful nature in the sight of God (Psalm 51:5; Romans 3:23; 5:12; 7:7-20). The first step toward understanding biblical evangelism is to understand the sinful nature of man. It is also necessary to understand the holy nature of God's law. The Bible has much more to say about the law than it does the gospel. The Bible has much more to say about God's judgment than it does about God's love. If the evangelistic message is consistent in expressing the biblical message to others, then more time must be devoted to preaching and teaching God's judgment and His law. If people do not understand God's law and His judgment, they will not be convicted of their sin nature which they cannot change or their sinful acts which they naturally cannot improve. If they are not convicted of their sin they will have no need to hear and understand the gospel.

One of my seminary professors, Dr. John Gerstner, determined that there are four ways to do evangelism.

Sacraments is the method used by the Roman Catholics and other sacerdotal churches.

Sell is the method used by the Arminians.

.

Shrug is the method (non-method) used by the liberals.

Seeking is the method used by many early reformed Christians especially by the great reformed thinker Jonathan Edwards.

The Puritan concept of evangelism known as "seeking" is the biblical form of evangelism I recommend. Jonathan Edwards left the church with profound words on the biblical doctrine of evangelism, but first a few words about the nature and scope of evangelism.

The "evangel" is the good news of the message of the redemptive work of Christ. When we add "ism" to evangel then we adopt as a world and life view the salvation message of Jesus Christ as we find it in the Word of God.

Who is responsible for the work of evangelism? In the New Testament, all Christians were involved in the task of evangelism (Acts 8:4, 5). Some proclaim the gospel as ordained ministers and laymen share the gospel in the providence of God. Those called by God to the ministry of the Word have a primary responsibility to do the work of an evangelist. However, every Christian has the responsibility to engage in the evangelistic enterprise. Christians evangelize by what they say and how they live in a fallen world. God is the Evangelist par excellence. He gave us the evangel and He gives us the opportunity to present the evangel, but He alone can grant new life.

Jonathan Edwards left the church with a legacy which has all but been forgotten. The legacy was a biblical view of evangelism, a God-centered evangelism known as seeking. I know many Christians who are enamored by the evangelistic work of Billy

Graham. I appreciate Mr. Graham and am convinced that he loves the Lord and wants to serve the Lord with all his heart. His preaching was uniquely simple and he communicated the gospel with fervor and conviction. However, I am troubled with his evangelism at one point. Mr. Graham apparently believes that an unconverted sinner can cause God to change the sinner's heart. Jonathan Edwards took the view that God could cause the heart to be changed and then the converted sinner could believe. Jonathan Edwards on his remarks *Concerning Efficacious Grace* wrote that "It is manifest that the Scripture supposes, that if ever men are turned from sin, God must undertake it, and he must be the doer of it; that it is his doing that must determine the matter..." (*The Works of Jonathan Edwards*, vol. 2, p. 543). Edwards believed that God acted to renew the will because the individual sinner could not cause the will of God to change. Only God the Holy Spirit could cause the will of man to change so that the sinner could believe and repent. This is commonly called "being born again." Later in the same treatise Edwards says, "In efficacious grace we are not merely passive, nor yet does God do some and we do the rest. But God does all, and we do all. God produces all, and we act all. For that is what he produces, viz. our own acts. God is the only proper author and fountain; we only are the proper actors..." (*The Works of Jonathan Edwards*, vol. 2, p. 557). You can see that Edwards believed that man acted because of God's doing. The difference, on this issue, between Jonathan Edwards and Billy Graham is that Mr. Graham believes that man can do something which will cause God to act. One reference in Scripture is sufficient to see who does what. "And a certain woman named Lydia, from the city of Thyatira, a seller of purple fabrics, a worshiper of God, was listening; and the Lord opened her heart to heed the things spoken by Paul" (Acts 16:14). Read it slowly and notice who did what to make who believe what. It was not the gospel message that changed the heart of Lydia. It was not Lydia's faith that changed her heart. It was not a sinner's prayer that changed her heart. It was the Lord that changed her heart, so that Lydia could believe the gospel. Also notice that she was "seeking" God before the Lord changed her heart.

The evangelistic message and method is either God-centered or man-centered. God-centered evangelism recognizes that man is spiritually dead and blind. Man is unable to produce new life by his own power. God-Centered evangelism proclaims that Christ died to save His people (Matthew 1:21). It is the Holy Spirit that regenerates the unbelieving sinner and grants the regenerated sinner the ability to believe, repent and obey. The sinner is saved by the grace of God. Man-centered evangelism teaches that man is not spiritually dead, but has the spark of divinity within the soul to do something to be saved. Man-centered evangelism teaches that Christ died to make salvation possible but the power of salvation remains in the hands of the sinner to make a decision to believe. Man-centered evangelism leaves the decision in the hands of the sinner. Is God sovereign or is man sovereign? Does man trust in his own ability or the gracious hand of God? An understanding of the authority and sovereignty of God is the basis upon which the professing Christian will develop the message and method of evangelism.

Although using doctrinal name tags is often considered offensive, it is necessary for classification. Arminian evangelism refers to man-centered evangelism. Calvinistic evangelism refers to God-centered evangelism. The reasons for an affinity to Arminian evangelism are many. Arminian evangelism was popularized in America by Charles Finney (1792-1875) and his followers particularly using man-made methods, rather than following the biblical doctrine. From my experience in church work over the past thirty years, I believe the overwhelming majority of evangelical Christians believe and practice Arminian evangelism. It is called man-centered evangelism because it makes man the cause of salvation.

The Synod of Dort (1618-1619) was called into session to settle the controversy between the followers of Jacob Arminius and his doctrine and the followers of John Calvin and his doctrine. These two opposing doctrines in the evangelical church are known as Arminianism and Calvinism. Arminian evangelism teaches that the unconverted sinner is able to believe and repent. Regeneration takes place because the sinner believes. Calvinistic evangelism teaches that man is not able to believe until God regenerates the heart. Arminianism teaches that "God, as far as He is concerned, wished to bestow equally upon all people the benefits which are gained by Christ's death; but that the distinction by which some rather than others come to share in the forgiveness of sins and eternal life depends on their own free choice..." (*Canons of Dort*, Second Main Point of Doctrine, Section VI). Calvinism teaches that "the fact that some receive from God the gift of faith within time, and that others do not, stems from his eternal decision" (*The Canons of Dort*, The First Main Point of Doctrine, Article 6). Arminians teach that man makes the decision (often called the sinners prayer or some other pragmatic, but unbiblical tool). Calvinism teaches that God makes the decision.

Arminianism teaches that "unregenerate man is not strictly or totally dead in his sins or deprived of all capacity for spiritual good but is able to hunger and thirst for righteousness or life and to offer the sacrifice of a broken and contrite spirit which is pleasing to God" (*Canons of Dort*, The Third and Fourth Main Points of Doctrine, Section IV). Calvinism teaches that "all people are conceived in sin and are born children of wrath, unfit for any saving good, inclined to evil, dead in their sins, and slaves to sin; without the grace of the regenerating Holy Spirit they are neither willing nor able to return to God, to reform their distorted nature, or even to dispose themselves to such reform" (*Canons of Dort*, The Third and Fourth Main Points of Doctrine, Article 3). If men are dead in sin and not willing to return to God, then nothing that person can say, do, or think will cause his or her salvation. Just as Rome errs with baptismal regeneration, evangelicals err with decisional regeneration.

The reasons for so much deviant evangelistic activity among evangelicals are too many and too complicated for the purpose of this brief manuscript. However, the fundamental cause of so much error in evangelistic endeavors in our day can be traced to Bible institutes, Christian liberal arts colleges, Bible colleges, seminaries and other training centers for Christian workers. Many of these organizations, not under the authority of the church, err by teaching unbiblical evangelistic doctrine and practice. They also propagate the idea that evangelism is the primary duty of Christians. When a young Christian develops a passion for some aspect of religion, it is difficult to re-channel those passions in another direction. These institutions seem to overlook the more important mandate - the mandate to worship God. If Christians search the

Scriptures carefully and diligently, they will learn that worship is a predominant mandate throughout the Old Testament and the New Testament. They will not only learn that they must worship God, they will learn how to worship Him.

The Arminian approach to evangelism encourages people to join the church who may be unconverted. How terrible to lead people to think they may be converted when they may or may not be converted. Baptism, praying at the altar in a church, praying "the sinner's prayer" or any other activity on the part of an unconverted sinner will not produce salvation. God and God alone can empower the person to repent and believe. The Bible issues the commandment to "believe on the Lord Jesus Christ." If someone obeys the commandment, it is because the Holy Spirit renewed the soul with new life. A person may say, "I repent and believe many things about the Lord Jesus Christ," but until God creates a new heart in him or her, salvation is not possible. Nevertheless, encourage everyone to seek the Lord while He may be found. Then ask the unconverted sinner to believe on the Lord Jesus and receive and rest in Him as Lord and Savior.

So what must the evangelist do so that the unconverted sinner will seek God? Tell him or her to read the Bible and to attend Bible studies. Explain the law and the gospel. Tell him or her to seek the Lord while He may be found. They can seek the Lord by being present for the preaching and teaching of the Word of God, obey His commandments, and ask God's people to pray for his or her conversion. Now I can imagine someone may say, "You will not get many church members that way." True! But is the goal to get church members or is it to obey everything that Christ has commanded?

God created His people to worship Him. They cannot worship Him unless they love Him and obey His commandments. One commandment out of hundred's of His commandments is to "Make disciples of all nations. . .teaching them to observe all that I commanded you..." (Matt. 28:19-20).

Principles of Reformation and Revival

The first principle of reformation and revival is the return to biblical authority. Reformation is a biblical concept that begins with the discovery or in some situations the recovery of the truth found in the Word of God. The recovery of truth was significantly important in the 16th century reformation. Reformation was the recovery of the cardinal doctrines. Revival follows reformation when the church practices biblical doctrine. In a word it was a recovery of biblical truth. When biblical truth is restored then the doors of heaven will be open to revival. Revival will not take place unless truth is brought into the Christian experience. What truth does the church need to recover?

The church needs to recover or discover the authority upon which doctrinal or theological assertions may be debated. The Latin phrase often used in the 16th century Reformation is *sola scriptura* which means "by Scripture alone." Scripture is the final authority to teach people what they must believe about God and what God expects of them. The English speaking world stands on the precipice of a neo-dark age because "Scripture alone" is no longer the final authority in the Protestant church. The liberal theologians teach their students one gospel while the fundamentalists another gospel. The antinomians preach one gospel, while the legalists preach another gospel. The Calvinists preach one gospel, while the Arminians preach another gospel. The list of different gospels is endless! The Bible explains the gospel and it is only one gospel!

Until the differences are resolved, reformation will never take place. Therefore, the church will not experience revival. First, the individual Christian must resolve any internal struggles with the truth of the gospel found in the full counsel of God. Once the truth of the gospel is recovered to the mind of an individual Christian, then reformation and revival may spread throughout the church.

The second principle of reformation and revival is salvation by grace alone. The 16th century reformer, Martin Luther, struggled bitterly with the theological concepts commonly referred to as "bondage and freedom." His flair for individualism provoked an internal battle, because despite his effort to free himself from sin, he found himself imprisoned to guilt and sin. His study of the book of Romans revealed the answer. It was justification by faith alone. But how did he obtain this declaration of freedom? Luther said it was, *sola gratia*, by grace alone.

During the 16th and 17th centuries, the evangelical church realized and acknowledged that salvation came forth from an eternal and sovereign God and His inscrutable will was worthy of absolute trust for eternal salvation. Today the evangelical church has changed its theology and placed part of the process of salvation in the hands of fallen human beings. Like the Roman church of the 16th century, the majority of the evangelical church of the 20th century teaches that humans can, at least, cooperate in their salvation. The giants of classical Christianity have always taught that the human is enslaved to sin and Satan, until God takes the initiative and by His grace alone gives new life so that the human will can respond to the call of the gospel. Yes, every person is born equal. At birth we are depraved sinners and just like the corpse at the mortuary, we are unable to raise ourselves from the dead. We are given new life, *sola gratia*, by grace alone. "For by grace you have been saved through faith; and that not of yourselves, it is a gift of God; not as a result of works, that no one should boast" (Eph. 2:8, 9). God does not run a democracy. His government is not "of the people, by the people, and for the people." His government is absolute, sovereign, benevolent, and eternal. Trust God, because He alone can free you from your prison and give you eternal life.

Every Christian should actively engage these two principles of reformation and revival in their personal lives.

Scripture alone.
Salvation by grace alone.

Every pastor, preacher, and teacher ought to preach these principles. The centrality of these reformation principles are found in the Word of God. If professing Christians deny them, the church will continue its spiritual decline. If Christians embrace them, the church will be reformed by the Word of God.

There are several examples of reformation in the redemptive history of the Old Testament Church. One of them occurred during the reign of Josiah (2 Chronicles 34 and 35). Those two chapters in 2 Chronicles should be read with great care.

The Bible indicates that Josiah "did right in the sight of the Lord, and walked in the ways of his father David..." (2 Chronicles 34:2). King David was the standard for the life and faith of all succeeding kings in Judah. The Bible says Josiah was seeking God which is the way to reformation. Josiah purged Judah and Jerusalem of pagan and false worship. During the process there was a cleansing of the temple and the high priest discovered "the book of the law." In the 18th year of Josiah's reign he ordered Shaphan the scribe,

Maaseiah the governor, and Joah the recorder to repair the house of the Lord. When these men consulted Hilkiah the high priest, he reported that he had found the Book of the Law of the Lord given by Moses. If Hilkiah had not been busy working for reformation, he would not have found the Bible. The king gathered all the elders of Judah and Jerusalem, with all the people of Judah and Jerusalem, both great and small to hear the reading of the Word of God. The reformation that occurred in Judah during the reign of Josiah lasted throughout his lifetime (2 Chronicles 34:33).

A reformation will cause a lively revival when Christians are being reformed by the Word of God and receiving Christ by grace through faith alone. The challenge to every Christian is to be a reformer according to the Word of God.

Conclusion

J. Gresham Machen said, "The absence of doctrinal teaching and preaching is certainly one of the causes for the present lamentable ignorance in the church." Dr. Machen went on to say, "doctrine is intellectual, and Christians are generally anti-intellectual. Doctrine is ivory tower philosophy, and they scorn ivory towers.... It is a fundamental, theoretical mistake of practical men to think that they can be merely practical, for practice is always the practice of some theory" (*Education, Christianity and the State*). It is sad but true that many churchmen think that teaching and preaching from a sound theological foundation is theoretical.

A theological belief system (and everyone has a theological belief system) will effect how one thinks, acts, and performs. Modernist believe that theology is like a novelty shop where one may find all sorts of unusual goodies, but often these novelties are disguised as the real thing. Truth and accuracy in interpretation will expose the false covering, but it requires hard work and patience. The evangelical church in our country has been plagued with a smorgasbord of theology and Christian philosophy for several generations and we need not expect to see a correction come easily or quickly. The place to begin is with the essence of Christian doctrine.

The rational mind understands according to the perspectives and yes the presuppositions of a total belief system. For instance, I cannot gather any knowledge and sort out that knowledge in my mind without bringing many other ideas, facts, and data in the full picture. To claim to be able to do otherwise will cause some flirting with ancient Greek philosophies like Gnosticism and Stoicism.

We derive our theological system from the Bible, but we are not the Bible. We are fallible human beings who interpret the Bible using all the resources that God gives in this fallen world. Our theology is not a belief system without the influence of common grace, but Holy Scripture must regulate belief and practice as we are empowered by the Holy Spirit to discover the nature and character of God.

About the Author

Martin Murphy has a B.A. in Bible from Columbia International University and Master of Divinity from Reformed Theological Seminary. Martin spent nearly thirty years in the class room, the pulpit, the lectern, the study, and the library. He now devotes most of his time consolidating academic and practical gains by writing books. He and his wife Mary live in Dothan, Alabama. He is the author of fourteen Christian books.

The Church: First Thirty Years, 344 pages, ISBN 9780985618179, $15.95. This book is an exposition of the Book of Acts. It will help Christians understand the purpose, mission, and ministry of the church.

The Dominant Culture: Living in the Promised Land, 172 pages, ISBN 970991481118, $11.95. This book examines the culture of Israel during the period of the Judges. It explains how worldviews influence the church and it reveals biblical principles to help Christians learn how to live in the culture.

My Christian Apology, 98 pages, ISBN 9780984570874, $7.95. This book investigates the doctrine of Christian apologetics. It explains rational Christian apologetics.

Return to the Lord, 130 pages, ISBN 9780984570805, $8.95. This book is an exposition of Hosea. The prophet speaks a message of repentance and hope. Hosea's prophetic message to Old Testament and New Testament congregations is, "you have broken God's covenant; return to the Lord." Dr. Richard Pratt said, "We need more correct and practical instruction in the prophetic books, and you have given us just that."

Theological Terms in Layman Language, 130 pages, ISBN 9780985618155, $8.95. This book was written so that simple words like faith or not so simple words like aseity are explained in plain language. Theological Terms in Layman Language is easy to read and designed for people who want a brief definition for theological terms. The terms are in layman friendly language.

Brief Study of the Ten Commandments, 164 pages, 9780991481163, $10.95. This book will help Christians discover or re-discover the meaning of the Ten Commandments.

The Present Truth, 164 pages, ISBN 9780983244172, $8.95. Each chapter examines a topic relative to the Christian life. Topics such as church, sin, anger, marriage, education and more.

Doctrine of Sound Words: Summary of Christian Theology, 423 pages, ISBN 9780991481125, $16.95. This is a book of Christian doctrine in topical format. It covers a wide range of theological topics such as, the triune God, creation, providence, sin, justification, repentance, Christian liberty, free will, marriage and divorce, Christian fellowship, et al). There are thirty three topics beginning with "Holy Scriptures" and ending with "The Last Judgment." It is a systematic theology for laymen based on the full counsel of God.

Friendship: The Joy of Relationships, ISBN 9780986405518, 48 pages, $6.49. This is the kind of book that friends give each other and share the principles with each other. If friends do not feel comfortable sharing these relationship principles with each other, the friendship may not really exist. Friendship involves a relationship of distinction. It is a relationship that respects the dignity of another person. The Bible teaches a different version of what it means to be a friend than the popular culture teaches. There are many occasions when friends say they are friends, but they are not friends. "Even my own familiar friend in whom I trusted, who ate my bread, has lifted up his heel against me" (Psalm 41:9). A true friend will endure and sacrifice for a friend. "A friend loves at all times" (Proverbs 17:7) and "there is a friend who sticks closer than a brother" (Proverbs 18:24).

Ultimate Authority for the Soul, ISBN 9780986405501, 151 pages, $9.99. What is the ultimate authority for human beings? This book examines that question and concludes that every rational being has some recognition of God as the ultimate authority. Although God is the ultimate authority, He confers His authority by means of the Word of God. The author examines Psalm 119 to build a defense for the ultimate authority for the soul. Although this book was written for Christians, the author builds the case that authority is a principle necessary to maintain sanity and order in the family, the church and civil society. The Word of God connects the soul with reality.